BLAZING THE TRAIL

BLAZING THE TRAIL

Where is the Holy Spirit leading the Church?

Peter Hocken

Bible *alive!*

First published in 2001 by Bible Alive Ltd.
Graphic House, 124 City Road
Stoke-on-Trent ST4 2PH

*© **2001 Peter Hocken***

*British Library Cataloguing-in-Publication Data. A
catalogue record for this book is available from
the British Library.*

ISBN 0 9540335 0 7

*Cover Design by Nick Mills
Arcus Design, Farnham, Surrey
01252 727929*

Contents

Foreword

I regard it as a particular joy to have been asked to pen the foreword of Fr Peter Hocken's latest writing. Fr Peter has been a friend and mentor since my seminary days and I have been privileged over the years to share and discuss many of the insights he has brought together in this book. Its contents are a rich distillation of many years of prayer and study, and of reflective observation of the various movements of renewal in the Churches in general and in the Roman Catholic Church in particular. I have always found Peter's thought exciting and incisive, and of great benefit, both in my spiritual life as well as in my priesthood and ministry. This new book is no exception.

Following the Great Jubilee of the year 2000, there are many hopes and expectations in the Church. In the western world, such hope is the fruit of the Holy Spirit in the midst of apparently discouraging signs. For how, in fact, do we describe the present state of the Church? It is not easy to steer a path between, on the one hand, a cheery optimism for the future that refuses any recognition or responsibility for the present ills of the Church and, on the other, a sense of depression and discouragement leading to analyses that see solutions elsewhere than in the essential proclamation of the Gospel message. Navigating such a path is itself a work of the Holy Spirit.

The basis of all our confidence is the great mystery of God's plan of salvation, revealed in the first coming of Jesus Christ and to be fully manifested and realised at his second coming. At the same time, discouragement and failure have their roots in sin and in losing sight of the fundamental elements of that mystery of our salvation. There is a need for repentance and conversion and a lively penetration of God's full purpose - including a rediscovery of those elements that have perhaps gone out of focus.

Peter Hocken's new book marvellously combines all of these qualities. You will enjoy a renewed sense of engagement with the mysteries of our faith, and will be invited into relationship with the persons of the Trinity and with the life-giving proclamation of the message of the gospel. You will sense the movement from gospel to mystery as you enter into the mystagogia – the mysteries of the sacramental life of the Church.

You will be challenged into thinking about aspects of God's plan of salvation that have not always figured strongly on our horizons – the place of Israel in God's plan, the initial proclamation of gospel leading to a personal conversion to Christ, and the challenge of making our own the longing of the Spirit and Bride for the second coming of the Lord.

The Holy Father has firmly placed repentance as the condition for the new springtime in the life of the Church. He has spoken of repentance for the attitudes, throughout history, held by sons and daughters of the Church towards Jews or towards Christians of other denominations; in addition, he speaks of repentance for a general indifference regarding the social or moral issues in society. Fr Peter has taken up these challenges and shows that such repentance will enable us to become more humble and open to learning from others.

My favourite part of this book is the section 'The Spirit makes the Church more Eucharistic'. It has given me a new insight into the nature of the priesthood. The priest is called to become conformed to Christ and Fr Peter describes this within the two dimensions of teaching and service. These two dimensions are expressed in the liturgy, in the liturgy of the word and especially the liturgy of the eucharist – word and action. Perhaps one of the great areas of renewal in the priestly life will be the rediscovery of the teaching ministry that is integral to the sacrament of Orders. Peter Hocken's book has challenged me to see teaching in its various dimensions, not simply as a gift that an individual priest may or may not possess, but rather an essential part of the priest's conformity to Christ.

Blazing the Trail has so much to offer. Its clarity, insights and challenges will convince you that the Spirit is speaking to you. It is a truly prophetic vision and a source for great encouragement.

Fr Paul J Watson, S.T.L.
Director Maryvale Institute, Birmingham

Introduction

In the autumn of 1998 I received an invitation to conduct the annual charismatic retreat for priests and deacons at Leeds in Easter week 2000. This invitation provided the background for *Blazing the Trail*. It gave me an opportunity to do something I have had a growing desire to do: to reflect on the ways in which, in our day, the Holy Spirit is leading the Catholic Church towards the realisation of God's full purpose in his Son, Jesus Christ. Therefore I chose as the title for the retreat: Where is the Holy Spirit leading the Church? This may seem to be a presumptuous undertaking, and wide open to the danger of being highly subjective. It could be one priest's blueprint for what he would like to see happen in the Church, attributed to the Holy Spirit.

However, I am convinced that with the light of the Holy Spirit it is possible to read the signs of the times. I also believe that the danger of undue subjectivity is significantly reduced by the examination of three distinct sets of data: (i) the witness of the experience of the Holy Spirit in the charismatic renewal; (ii) a deeper searching of the sacred scriptures; and (iii) recent developments in the teaching of the magisterium of the Catholic Church, that is, the teaching of the Pope and the bishops. The first is not as subjective as critics and non-participants in the charismatic movement may think: for after more than thirty years there is a considerable body of objective evidence as to the fruit of charismatic renewal in the lives of Catholics and other Christians. The deeper searching of the scriptures is part of every authentic movement of renewal and it is the heart of all Christian theology.[1] Further, the magisterium 'is not superior to the Word of God, but is its servant.'[2] In the renewal of the Catholic Church in the last half of the twentieth century, the teachings of the magisterium have become much more biblical in their inspiration and their expression, as I hope this book will show.

Perhaps the most convincing ground for the positions presented in this book is the confluence between these three sources. I use the word 'confluence' rather than 'identity', because the evidence from the three sources is convergent rather than identical. In some areas renewal movements are pioneering the way, and the magisterium, while generally moving in the same direction, is watching and discerning before fully endorsing the pioneers. In other areas, the magisterium is leading the way, and the renewal movements need to listen and receive this expression of the Word of God.

The empirical data in this book largely come from the charismatic renewal. But many of the same elements are also evident in the host of new movements that have been such a prominent feature in the life of the Catholic Church in the last half of the twentieth century. I believe that the charismatic renewal has a particular significance as a stream of life from on high: it has no one human founder and has sprung up in almost every Christian tradition. But it is not the only current of the Holy Spirit, and it needs to be seen and to see itself alongside other currents of renewal as a particular impulse of the Holy Spirit for the renewal of the whole Church.

I see this confluence, that is not identity, as perfectly right and normal in the life of the Church. For the Church is a living organism with pulsating currents of life, with a multiplicity of organs, limbs, tendons and nerves, with areas of strength and areas of weakness. The currents of renewal are not the Church. They exist for the Church. They are for the *life* of the Church. They lead to revitalised expressions of faith served by renewed forms of ministry, and fleshed out in a renewed liturgy, encouraged, sustained and fine-tuned by the magisterium and interaction with the wider Church.

The Holy Spirit's work of renewal touches the whole of God's creation, the whole of God's revelation and every dimension of the life of the Church. Enthusiastic charismatics can easily focus narrowly on one or two areas that are more obviously 'spiritual'. It is true that God does not usually address all dimensions at once. But God has a strategy and has priorities. While God typically begins with areas that are most crucial as a personal foundation, he then leads believers into other and wider areas, so that nothing created and therefore loved by the Creator is left outside his renewing purpose.

In looking at this global work of renewal, I have singled out four areas where I have seen major new developments or changes in direction in recent decades.

These four topics correspond to the four morning talks of the Leeds retreat, preceded on the opening evening by a talk on the Holy Spirit making the Church more Trinitarian. If I had had more time, I would probably have added a talk on the Holy Spirit making the Church more earthy, more incarnate in the life of the world as a witness to the coming kingdom in the midst of human pain and suffering. For there is no doubt that in recent decades the Catholic Church has come to see the transformation of society, along with the promotion of justice and peace, as intrinsic to her mission, inseparable from the making of Christ present by the power of the Holy Spirit.

Since the material in this book was prepared as a retreat for Catholic priests and deacons, I refer throughout to the Church when talking about the Catholic Church in communion with Rome. But in the post-Vatican II era, the Catholic Church recognises that the other Christian churches and ecclesial communities are within the household of faith, and not outside it. The Holy Spirit cannot be leading the other Christian traditions in a totally different direction from the Catholic Church. I believe, in fact, that the same signs can be found in the other Christian communions: the Holy Spirit making them more evangelistic, more eucharistic, more ecumenical and more eschatological. But the forms these signs take vary, and the historical obstacles in the way of renewal are different from one tradition to another. I hope that the sisters and brothers of other Christian churches and traditions who read this book will recognise the same leadings of the Holy Spirit in their own communions.

Pope John Paul II has certainly been a trail-blazer. In his letter, *Tertio millennio adveniente,* to prepare the Catholic Church for the new millennium, Pope John Paul II said that 'the whole of Christian history appears to us as a single river, into which many tributaries pour their waters.'[3] This image gives a powerful sense of the Church in history moving towards her destiny in the kingdom of God. My prayer is that *Blazing the Trail* will help many to have a stronger sense of this direction, and with it a new hope for the future that is God's gift through the Holy Spirit.

Peter Hocken
January 2001

Chapter One

The Holy Spirit makes the Church more Trinitarian

One memory of my early days in the priesthood is of the reluctance of many priests to preach on the Trinity. The feast of the Most Holy Trinity, a week after Pentecost, was an occasion when priests least liked to preach. The general sentiment was that the Trinity is a mystery, too complicated for ordinary people to handle, and best left as a mystery without explanation and beyond comprehension.

For many of us, experience of the renewing work of the Holy Spirit has radically changed this attitude. A deeper coming of the Holy Spirit has opened up our lives to the inner dynamic of the Trinity: the Holy Spirit relates us to the Father and to the Son and we find our personal identity in relation to the Father, the Son and the Holy Spirit.

The Holy Spirit reveals God as our personal Father. I come to know what it means that I am a son of God or a daughter of God. 'For all who are led by the Spirit of God are sons of God. For you did not receive the spirit of slavery to fall back into fear, but you have received the spirit of sonship. When we cry "Abba, Father!" it is the Spirit himself bearing witness with our spirit that we are children of God, and if children, then heirs, heirs of God and fellow heirs with Christ' (Rom. 8:14-17). Through the Spirit we can cry out 'Abba, Father'; 'Almighty God, you are my Father, you are our Father.' As God's sons and daughters, we have the freedom and the ability to approach the Father, to enter into his holy presence: 'for through him [Jesus] we both have access in one Spirit to the Father' (Eph. 2:18).

To be sons and daughters of God is to be enlivened, inspired and moved by the Spirit of God. I can experience the new life pulsating within me. Not all the time, for there are times when I feel nothing, and then I have to act in faith, knowing that the Spirit of God is in me. But there are times when I do experience the guidance of the Spirit. I know that I was led to talk to this person, to speak this word, to do this act of kindness, through the leading of the Holy Spirit. These experiences increase our desire to live every moment as a faithful son or daughter of the Father.

The Holy Spirit reveals Jesus of Nazareth to be the Messiah of Israel, the Saviour of the world, the Lord of all and the Son of God. Jesus tells Peter that he could only make the confession, 'You are the Christ, the Son of the living God', by revelation from the Father in heaven (Matt. 16:16-17). Paul tells us, 'Therefore I want you to understand that no one speaking by the Spirit of God ever says "Jesus be cursed!" and no one can say "Jesus is Lord" except by the Holy Spirit' (1 Cor. 12:3). The revealing work of the Holy Spirit is further described in the Gospel of John. Jesus tells his disciples about the Holy Spirit: 'He will glorify me, for he will take what is mine and declare it to you. All that the Father has is mine; therefore I said that he will take what is mine and declare it to you' (John 16:14-15).

Experientially, when we receive the Holy Spirit to be the living force of our spirits, we come to a knowledge of Jesus as Saviour, Lord and Son of God. Having our sins forgiven, we live in the sphere of Jesus' rule: 'He has delivered us from the dominion of darkness and transferred us to the kingdom of his beloved Son, in whom we have redemption, the forgiveness of sins' (Col. 1:13-14). To live under Jesus' rule is to live according to his Spirit. It is to live in submission to Jesus, through whose glorious humanity the Spirit of God is ever being poured out in abundance. It is to live in loving obedience to Jesus and thereby always to be receiving afresh the Holy Spirit as the source of our thoughts, energies and activities.

As we open ourselves to the Holy Spirit, we pay more attention to the role of the Holy Spirit in the life of Jesus. We see how his public ministry only began after the Holy Spirit descended on him at his baptism. 'Jesus, full of the Holy Spirit, returned from the Jordan, and was led by the Spirit' (Luke 4:1). In fact, he was led into the desert for forty days of temptation. We also find that when we are filled with the Holy Spirit, we come under attack and are tempted in a way we had not known before. We see the connection between Jesus' baptism and his works of power. After Pentecost, the apostles understood this: Peter tells Cornelius and his household 'how God anointed Jesus of Nazareth with the Holy Spirit and with power; how he went about doing good and healing all that were oppressed by the devil, for God was with him' (Acts 10:38). We also pay more attention to the prayer of Jesus, and its trinitarian character: how Jesus prayed to the Father, and how 'he rejoiced in the Holy Spirit' as he addressed the Father (Luke 10:21).

The Church's trinitarian consciousness

At the same time as the charismatic renewal and other currents of spiritual renewal have been restoring a trinitarian awareness to many believers, the Holy Spirit has been restoring a greater trinitarian consciousness at all levels within the Church. This has happened especially through the work of the Second Vatican Council in encouraging and promoting the renewal in Catholic biblical studies and the liturgical movement. The structure of liturgical prayer is itself trinitarian, being most typically addressed to the Father through Christ our Lord in the power and unity of the Holy Spirit: 'We make this prayer through Jesus Christ, your Son our Lord, who lives and reigns with You in the unity of the Holy Spirit, one God, for ever and ever.' The new eucharistic prayers make more plain the role of the Holy Spirit in making the person of the Lord Jesus present, first in the eucharistic elements and then in those who eat the body of the Lord and drink of his blood.[1]

A strong impulse towards a greater Trinitarian emphasis was given by Pope John Paul II when he called for the three years immediately preceding the Great Jubilee of the year 2000 to be devoted to reflection on the three persons of the Trinity. 'The thematic structure of this three-year period, centred on Christ, the Son of

4

God made man, must necessarily be theological, and therefore trinitarian' (TMA, para. 39). Thus 1997 was devoted to the person of Christ, 1998 to the Holy Spirit and 1999 to God the Father.

Recent documents from Rome show much more of a trinitarian structure and awareness than comparable documents that came out before Vatican II. This Trinitarian structure of the Christian life can be clearly illustrated in the Catechism of the Catholic Church. Apart from the section explicitly devoted to the Trinity (paras 232-267),[2] there are other important sections which reflect the trinitarian structure of Church life. The section on Christ includes the heading 'The Resurrection - a work of the Holy Trinity' (paras 648 - 650).[3] A section on the Church is headed, 'The Church - people of God, body of Christ, temple of the Holy Spirit'.[4] This treatment indicates that it is not just that the Church believes in the mystery of the Trinity. The Church has a Trinitarian shape and structure. Because the Church has been created by the sharing of life by the triune God, all Christians share in the communion of the blessed Trinity precisely as they are bonded together as Church.

The trinitarian structure of the Church and all Christian life is further shown by the Catechism's teaching on the liturgy. The first chapter on the sacraments treats of 'The paschal mystery in the age of the Church' and has as title for its first article, 'The liturgy - work of the Holy Trinity'.[5] This article has three sections: 'The Father - source and goal of the Liturgy', 'Christ's work in the liturgy' and 'The Holy Spirit and the Church in the liturgy'. Here again we find that the rediscovery of the role of the Holy Spirit brings everything alive. The Holy Spirit is the Lord and giver of life. So the Catechism has sub-headings for the role of the Holy Spirit: the Holy Spirit prepares for the reception of Christ, the Holy Spirit recalls the mystery of Christ, the Holy Spirit makes present the mystery of Christ, and the communion of the Holy Spirit.[6]

The Holy Spirit is the dynamism, the torrent of life that touches us, that stirs us, that communicates Jesus to us, that unites us to him and to one another, that lifts us up in worship and adoration of God, that drives us forth in mission and service. 'The Holy Spirit is like the sap of the Father's vine which bears fruit on its branches' (CCC, para. 1108). The sap flows. It rises up. It surges through the branches and the stems of the vine.

The Holy Spirit does not only make our faith alive. The Holy Spirit brings God to us. That is, through the Holy Spirit we are inserted into Christ, into his death, and so we enter into the communion of the Holy Trinity. The Holy Spirit brings every aspect of our faith alive, and properly relates each element to every other element. The Holy Spirit brings life, makes us one, makes us coherent, and places us in the one body of Christ. But the pattern is always that we are conformed to Jesus in his death so that we can share in his resurrection.

The communion of many in one

The Church, made up of those who are reborn into the divine life of the Holy Trinity, is a communion of many persons in one life, of many members in one body, of many gifts in one gift, the Holy Spirit.[7] St Paul brings out the relationship between the Holy Trinity and this harmonious unity of one in many and many in one. 'Now there are varieties of gifts, but the same Spirit; and there are varieties of service, but the same Lord; and there are varieties of working, but it is the same God who inspires them all in every one' (1 Cor. 12:4-6). This emphasis on variety and unity is clearly deliberate, and Paul relates this multiplicity to each person of the Trinity. It is of the nature of God to create a great variety of creatures, endowing them with a great variety of capacities. But all comes from the One and, when rightly received, leads to the One; but the goal is not just the unity of the origin, but the union of the bridegroom and the bride, of Christ and redeemed humanity.

There is another passage in St Paul's writings that emphasises the elements that are single and unique: 'There is one body and one Spirit, just as you were called to the one hope that belongs to your call, one Lord, one faith, one baptism, one God and Father of us all, who is above all and through all and in all' (Eph. 4:4-6). One Father, one Lord, one Spirit; one body, one hope, one faith, one baptism; many gifts, many forms of service, many ways of working. The richness of God that is expressed in the communion of three divine persons overflows into creation, overflows into the Church. Rich diversity in wonderful harmony: that is God's vision for the Church. Is it what we experience in the Church? Is it what we as Church present to the world?

The Trinitarian structure of Christian life

The work of the Holy Spirit then reveals the trinitarian structure of God, the trinitarian structure of the Church, the trinitarian structure of the liturgy, the trinitarian structure of Christian ministry, the trinitarian structure of Christian prayer, indeed the trinitarian structure of all Christian life. I use the word 'structure' because structure conveys an ordering framework, something more permanent. However, most structures we know have an impersonal character, whereas the 'structure of God' is wholly personal. God is wholly relational. There is nothing in God apart from the total inter-relationship of Father, Son and Holy Spirit. Since the whole work of salvation is the work of the Holy Spirit, every grace has, so to speak, a trinitarian shape. If God's grace is at work in anyone, they are being moved by the Spirit, drawn to Jesus and the fellowship in his body, and blessed by the Father. When we ask how we can teach the Trinity to our people, we should not think of the Trinity as a difficult doctrine foreign to them that we have to try and make meaningful or relevant. We must start from the fact that those who have been given the grace of the Lord already have a trinitarian reality within them. Our teaching in the Spirit will make sense of their experience of grace.

Renewed ministry

For those ordained to the ministry of priest or deacon, personal renewal through a conscious opening to the gift of the Holy Spirit is the key to a renewed ministry bearing the fruit of the Spirit. Let me share a little of my own experience that echoes that of many other ministers of the Lord.

It was in 1971, through what we now call the charismatic renewal, that I found a new depth of life in the Holy Spirit. For me, it was not at all dramatic, but the immediate effects were quite marked. I came into a small group of lay Catholics who were praising the Lord with great freedom and joy, and I sensed interiorly that I could enter in. This was how I received the gift of tongues. The most immediate effect was to discover the living Lordship of Jesus Christ. Of course I already believed that Jesus Christ is the only Lord and Saviour - but I saw now that as the living Lord, the risen-ascended Jesus guides us today. He speaks to us today, he protects us today. I could live in faith-dependence on him, receiving from him in the Spirit, allowing him to be my Lord now. This is the work of the Holy Spirit: to reveal Jesus, to unite us to Jesus, to communicate the mind and heart of Jesus to us.

This experience of the Spirit revealing the living Lordship of Jesus quickly affected the way I exercised my priestly ministry. My way of preparing sermons changed from being primarily an intellectual work at my desk to being a praying work in the chapel. The content changed too. From primarily popularising the latest theology, at that time often an explanation of Vatican II, I sought from the Lord what he wanted said to this congregation or group: for homilies, I sought this from the liturgical readings for the day, and for other talks, I sought the message and the scriptural passages to use. In this way, I discovered more fully what it means to be a minister of the Word of God. It is to be at the service of the Lord in his Word; to be ready to be the mouthpiece for his Word; to receive his Word from his Spirit.

To submit in faith to the living Lordship of Jesus through his Spirit is to discover the power of the Spirit in his Word: to discover that his Word has power to pierce hearts, to convict of sin, to speak to the inner person. Now there were distinctively visible fruits from the preaching: not simply people saying, 'That was interesting, Father' or 'Thank you for a nice sermon', but people reporting - not necessarily immediately - how the Word had impacted and changed their lives. It was not that sensational results followed my preaching! But certainly there were constant signs that a word had struck home, that a seed had been planted, that a door had been opened, that a barrier had been removed.

Another, though less immediate, consequence of my personal renewal in the Holy Spirit was that I became more aware of my identification with Jesus before the Father. This is most obvious for the priest in the celebration of the eucharist, where the identification extends to repeating the very words of the Saviour at the Last Supper. But it became clearer to me in times of ministry that, faced by the pain and misery of the afflicted, I have to seek the word of the Father, just as Jesus did, in the power of the same Spirit. It was this dimension of my experience that showed me the full trinitarian pattern of the Church's life and ministry.

Practical implications

This personal reflection can lead to the practical question: 'What difference should this trinitarian renewal make to my ministry as a priest or deacon?' The first point to emphasize is that the Christian faith is trinitarian by nature and the Church is trinitarian in its structure. If we are opening ourselves up to God, to his Word and to the movement of his Spirit, then we are being drawn more deeply into the trinitarian communion of the Church. We do not have to do anything extra to make it so.

Secondly, however, we can grow in our understanding and we can grow in our ability to *articulate* this understanding. We need, perhaps, to do two things: first, to reflect on our experience of renewal in the faith; secondly, to study the important recent documents of the magisterium that are organised in a trinitarian pattern.

Reflect on your personal experience: on the Holy Spirit as agent, inspiration, movement, direction, energy, power, guide and shaper; on how the person of the Lord has come alive, on the centrality of his death and resurrection, on how he has forgiven our sins, on his love and his call; on how we have come to the Father: 'He who has seen me has seen the Father' (John 14:9); on how the Our Father means more to us; on the Father's amazing love and mercy; also, perhaps, on the Father's discipline in treating us as sons, 'for what son is there whom his father does not discipline?' (Heb. 12:7).

The clearer we are on our own experience, the more clearly we will be able to speak of the Holy Trinity in a way that corresponds to the distinctive working of each divine person. We will speak of the Father who sends his Son and his Spirit. The Catechism speaks of 'the joint mission of the Son and the Spirit', saying that 'in their joint mission, the Son and the Holy Spirit are distinct but inseparable' (CCC, para. 689). When the Spirit is sent to us, 'this joint mission will be manifested in the children adopted by the Father in the body of his Son' (CCC, para. 690).

To read the Catechism, the General Directory on Catechesis and recent encyclicals can reinforce our grasp of the trinitarian pattern and structure of Christian life. It can teach us to think Trinity. To think: the Father, who creates, who sends, from whom all things come and to whom all things go; to think: Christ the Son, sent from the Father, Word of God, the way to the Father, the truth about the Father, the life that comes from the Father; to think: Holy Spirit, the finger of God, the executor of God's will and purposes, the giver of life, the instigator of all holy thoughts.

As we think Trinity and preach Trinity, the Trinity will be at work. Our people will recognise the divine persons in their experience of new life, in the liturgy, in their experience of forgiveness and reconciliation, in their experience of worship and prayer, in their experience of love and service, in their experience of pain and conso-lation.

Chapter Two

The Holy Spirit makes the Church more Evangelistic

I: The Spirit and the gospel

The Holy Spirit makes the Church more evangelistic by bringing the word of God to life within the Church. Only the Holy Spirit can do that. Bringing the word of God to life has many dimensions: making the scriptures come alive; causing the person of Jesus Christ, the Word made flesh, to become real for us; hearing the voice of the Lord in the scriptures, in the fellowship and in the teaching of the Church; sensing the echoes of God present in the beauty and the intricacy of creation.

This opening up of the word of God is a constant factor in the Christian experience of living faith. It is a central reality in all movements of spiritual renewal. It is evident in the charismatic renewal, it is evident in the Cursillo movement, the Focolari, the Foyers de Charité and the Community of St Egidio. It is the common experience of Christians being touched by the Spirit of God.

The word of God received

First, the Holy Spirit enables believers to hear the word of God. This 'hearing' is likely to take many forms. The most common feature will be light, new light on many aspects of the scriptures: new light on biblical incidents, new light on particular phrases or verses, new light on the behaviour of a biblical character. Sometimes words or phrases from the Bible will jump out at us. We may experience them as God's word addressed personally to us. Maybe we will see ourselves in the reactions of Gideon, in the behaviour of David, in the impulsiveness and impatience of Joab, in the fearfulness of Jonah, in the demands of the mother of the sons of Zebedee.

What is common to all these experiences is a communication from on high, light from the Lord. His Spirit is opening up his word to us so that it is not just a story or a teaching on paper, but a life-giving word we receive from our heavenly Father. The life-giving word may be as varied as the words of scripture: deeply challenging, through which our merciful Father convicts us of sin; or deeply comforting and encouraging such as the Father's words to Jesus, 'You are my beloved Son, with whom I am well pleased' (Luke 3:22).

When the Holy Spirit brings the word to life, there is always in some way a revelation of Jesus Christ. The Holy Spirit always points to Jesus. As Jesus said in John's Gospel: 'He [the Spirit] will glorify me, for he will take what is mine and declare it to you' (16:14). The scriptures coming alive are inseparable from Jesus coming alive. The Spirit reveals Jesus as 'the way, the truth and the life' (John 14:6): Jesus is the way to the Father; he is God's truth embodied; Jesus is life - he embodies the eternal life of communion with the Father in the Spirit.

So, when the Holy Spirit brings the word of God to life, we recognise the voice of the Good Shepherd, as Jesus promised: 'The sheep hear his voice' (John 10:3). This is the mark of the Christian living by the Spirit of God. We hear the voice of Jesus, we respond to that voice and we follow him. 'He calls his own sheep by name and leads them out. When he has brought out all his own, he goes before them and the sheep follow him, for they know his voice' (John 10:3-4). Jesus makes clear the link between recognising his voice and being a disciple. The disciple is not just one who keeps the general rules of the Church. The disciple is one who hears, indeed who hears his or her own name, and who obeys and follows.

The disciples' experience of the Holy Spirit opening up the scriptures was not primarily of the Lord giving them private messages, but of the Lord opening up his plan, his heart, for his creation and his people. Receiving the word of God is therefore above all receiving the heart of God, which is manifested in Jesus his Son. 'For it is the God who said, "Let light shine out of darkness", who has shone in our hearts to give the light of the knowledge of the glory of God in the face of Christ' (2 Cor. 4:6). The light shines in our hearts, and the result is knowledge of the glory of God revealed in the appearance of Jesus.

The word of God given out

When the Holy Spirit has brought the word of God to life in our hearts, we have the desire and the capacity to speak the word of God to others. Perhaps this is the surest test that we have received the word. The result of hearing the Lord is that we can speak the Lord. When the Holy Spirit brings the word to life, we have a message to give, a testimony to share. We see this pattern in our experience of renewal and, in recent times, we have seen an increasing number of Catholics so touched by the Holy Spirit. As with the apostles who received the Holy Spirit at Pentecost, the people of God become witnesses to the gospel. Through the renewing work of the Spirit, more and more Catholics are wanting to tell others about Jesus Christ and his saving work.

When we yield to the Spirit of God and gain a clarity about the good news of salvation, we have the desire to preach it. It is the Holy Spirit that gives this desire. So we find in the Acts of the Apostles that the twelve were transformed on the day of Pentecost. Those who heard them were astonished at the preaching of these uneducated men (Acts 4:13). But the apostles said: 'We are witnesses to these things, and so is the Holy Spirit whom God has given to those who obey him' (Acts 5:32).

The desire to share the word of God leads to many kinds of sharing. Personal sharing is a characteristic of charismatic groups. The Holy Spirit gives us experience of the Lord's love, mercy, protection and healing. Personal witness is an important element in evangelisation. It makes the gospel personal and turns a general theory into a particular love. That is why so often it is the personal testimony that touches the hearer. The convincing testimony is a sharing about Jesus, not a sharing about our feelings.

Then the Holy Spirit gives the desire and the capacity to preach the gospel publicly, a desire that is not restricted to priests and deacons. Schools of evangelism are being formed, new evangelistic teams and communities are developing in many countries and lay people are emerging with evident evangelistic gifts. In some places bishops are recognising gifted lay Catholics as evangelists, in the same way that others have been recognised for years as catechists. As the Holy Spirit makes the Church more evangelistic, we should expect the calling of evangelist to become more common and more widely recognised. In the New Testament, there were believers who were designated as evangelists: Philip, one of the seven on whom hands were laid by the apostles (Acts 7:5-6), is described as an evangelist in Acts 21:8, and evangelists are included in the list of ministries in Ephesians 4:11.[1]

Reflect on your own experience of the Holy Spirit and how it has led you to speak of Jesus and bear witness to him before others. Think of how an awakening of the Holy Spirit gave you something significant to say, and the desire to say it. Reflect on how this produced new fruit from your preaching and teaching. See how giving examples from your own faith-experience truly blesses and helps others on their walk of faith.

The good news of the gospel

What then is the good news, the gospel, that the Christian is to proclaim to the unbelieving world? What is the heart of the message that the Holy Spirit brings alive as the Church is renewed to become more evangelistic? First of all, the good news is that something wonderful has happened. Jesus of Nazareth has been raised from the dead. 'We bring you the good news that what God promised to our fathers, this he has fulfilled by raising Jesus' (Acts 13:32-33). The good news includes the consequences of this remarkable event. 'Let it be known to you therefore, brethren, that through this man forgiveness of sins is proclaimed to you, and by him every one that believes is freed from everything from which you could not be freed by the law of Moses' (Acts 13:38-39).

While the 'good news' of the gospel was first of all the act of God in raising Jesus from the dead, it was soon grasped that his death and resurrection together are the core of the good news.[2] So Paul describes the gospel in this way: 'that Christ died for our sins in accordance with the scriptures, that he was buried, that he was raised on the third day in accordance with the scriptures, and that he appeared to Cephas, then to the twelve' (1 Cor. 15:3-5). But the events of Christ's death and resurrection did not occur in a vacuum. This Jesus, who died and was raised to life, had been sent from the Father, born of a virgin, and filled with the Spirit of God to exercise his ministry as Messiah and Saviour. So we can understand the good news to mean the whole Jesus-event: the incarnation, the coming of the Saviour in human flesh,[3] and his human life and ministry, and especially their consummation in the death-resurrection-ascension of Jesus, which is the heart of the gospel.

The good news that centres on the resurrection of Jesus includes the gift of the Spirit that is the immediate fruit of the cross and the resurrection (see Acts

2:38). It also includes the promise of the fulness of salvation in the Lord's coming in glory and the resurrection of the dead, foreshadowed in the resurrection of Jesus. The good news is the whole message of salvation, foundationally accomplished in the cross and resurrection, and still to be fully realised in the coming of the kingdom.

Developments in Catholic teaching

Just as the Holy Spirit has been enabling Catholics to evangelise, so the Holy Spirit has been guiding the teachers of the Catholic Church. In this section, we will look at the significant developments in official Catholic teaching on evangelisation over the last thirty years.

In fact, evangelisation is a relatively new word on Catholic lips. Even at the Second Vatican Council (1962-65), the term 'evangelisation' was rarely used. It occurs primarily in the Decree on the Missionary Activity of the Church *(Ad gentes)*, where it means the proclamation of the gospel, especially by missionaries in places where the faith has not taken root.[4] The term came into regular Catholic usage in 1975 with the Apostolic Letter of Paul VI, *Evangelii nuntiandi*, which is the first authoritative Catholic teaching on this subject. This is a significant example of a papal document shaping Catholic language and practice. *Evangelii nuntiandi* brought evangelisation explicitly on to the post-conciliar Catholic agenda, leading to much discussion of the topic and gradually to increased practice. Later, Pope John Paul II coined the phrase 'the new evangelisation' to describe the challenge facing the Church in reawakening living faith among peoples traditionally Christian but now largely secularised in mentality.[5]

The emergence of the term 'evangelisation' into a prominent place in Catholic discussion and strategy is not just a new emphasis. It represents the Holy Spirit opening the Catholic Church to new understanding: to rediscovering the process of conversion and initiation, particularly to the distinctive stages within this process. The General Directory on Catechesis has a striking phrase - 'the pedagogy of God' - to describe this process, which is an expression of the Father's tender love in Christ.[6]

The elements of this transformation are all present in the teaching of Vatican II. One foundational element is the teaching of the Constitution on Divine Revelation *(Dei verbum)* that revelation is supremely of a person, of the incarnate Word, and not primarily of propositions. Revelation is above all the revelation of Jesus Christ, and only secondarily of doctrines about Christ. That is why the Church's proclamation is primarily of a person and an event: of Christ, and particularly of his death, resurrection from the dead and ascension to the Father.

A second element has been the Council's teaching concerning 'the hierarchy of truths'.[7] The Catholic Church recognised that some doctrines are more foundational than others. This is not saying that some doctrines are unimportant, so the Council does not use the language of 'primary' and 'secondary'. It says that doctrines 'vary in their relation to the foundation of the Christian faith'. This is crucial for the evangelistic work of the Church, because what is foundational is proclaimed first. In this context we can understand why the Council revived the ancient pattern of initiation into the

Church by several stages over a period, the process known as the catechumenate.[8]

In terms of evangelisation, the key developments in the teaching of the magisterium have been: (i) the recognition that there are distinct phases in the process of Christian initiation and formation; (ii) that there is a distinct phase at the beginning in which the gospel message is proclaimed and unbelievers are called to conversion. In order to avoid this chapter becoming too technical, the development of this official Catholic teaching is described in more detail in the Appendix. Here the principal elements alone are mentioned.

Phases or stages in Christian initiation

Both the Rite of Christian Initiation of Adults and the General Directory for Catechesis set out a series of phases or stages in the bringing of people to faith, baptism and a full participation in the life of the Catholic Church. The stages envisaged can be presented as follows (for precise citation of the documents, see the Appendix):

* Christian witness, dialogue and presence in charity (the background context)

* the proclamation of the gospel and the call to conversion

* the catechumenate (first thorough instruction and formation in the faith) leading to sacraments of initiation (baptism, confirmation, first communion)
* ongoing formation in the faith in the heart of the church community.

In this vision of Christian initiation, each stage contributes something essential to the formation of the new Christian. In this Catholic vision, each stage takes place in a church context. It is the witness of life of the church community that provides the framework for attraction to the faith. It is the members of the Church who announce the gospel message, which is the foundation of the faith of the Church. The catechetical formation introduces the person who has accepted the gospel to the way of life of the Christian community, and in particular to its worship, centred on the mystery of the eucharist.

The proclamation of the gospel: several of the church documents call this phase 'first' (primary) or 'initial proclamation'. This proclamation is aimed at producing an 'initial' conversion. The Catholic community is uncomfortable with the idea that 'conversion' is a once-and-for-all experience that is complete in itself. On the other hand, the documents make clear that this initial conversion involves a turning to Jesus Christ and a decision to follow him. The initial conversion is the beginning of faith that needs to be deepened throughout our lives. But there is a distinct point of beginning, a point of acceptance, of response, to the word of God proclaimed.

This proclamation is primarily the proclamation of Jesus Christ, of his person, of his saving death and resurrection, of his life and ministry. 'The subject of proclamation is Christ who was crucified, died and is risen: through him, is accomplished our full and authentic liberation from evil, sin and death; through him God bestows "new life" that is divine and eternal. This is the Good News which changes man and his history, and which all peoples have a right to hear' (John Paul II, *Redemptoris missio*, para. 44).

Answering a deep Catholic need

This work of the Holy Spirit in equipping Catholics to evangelise and in leading the Church's leaders to insist on a primary proclamation of the gospel answers a deep need of the Catholic Church. The Catholic Church has long attached and still attaches a great importance to Catholic education of the young; however, we have been witnessing a decreasing impact in this Catholic apostolate, at least in Western society. In this country, the statistics for Sunday mass attendance have shown a steady decline over the last twenty to thirty years.

Despite our massive efforts to provide Catholic education for as many Catholic children as possible, we are seeing a disastrous falling away from the faith. This catastrophic lapsation rate among young people is common to almost all the countries of Western Europe. Today we hardly even expect the youngsters in our secondary schools to be practising their faith. Years of teaching the Catholic faith to these young people seems to have had the opposite effect to what we hoped. Instead of being filled with faith, they seem to be inoculated against it. 'I've heard it all.' In societies that were wholly Catholic, this problem used to be more hidden, as young people absorbed many things of faith from their entire culture and the church environment. In those days, the schematic instructions in Catholic schools built upon something that children drank in from the lives of their families and their parishes. But in the secularised societies of Western Europe today, the lack has become a gaping wound, with the Church making minimal impact on generations of young people, including those who have been through the Catholic school system.

This decline has coincided with the Catholic Church's endeavour to implement the reforms of the Second Vatican Council. We have been through a period of reaction against the old-fashioned memorising of catechism answers, and this has led to widespread attempts to make RE more relevant and more attractive, through narrative and story, involvement in service and discussion and sharing. But these changes have not stemmed the leakage, and are in fact blamed by many conservative Catholics as the cause of the problem.

I believe that we can see the response of the Holy Spirit to this wound of the Church in the currents of spiritual renewal leading Catholics to evangelise and in the Church's recognition of the need for explicit proclamation. The answer cannot be found in professional solutions alone: in new programs, in teachers with more technical qualifications, in trying to make liturgies more interesting. In fact, both the old-fashioned methods and many of the newer methods in catechesis failed to understand that faith comes through response to a proclamation: 'So faith comes from what is heard, and what is heard comes by the preaching of Christ' (Rom. 10:17). This rediscovery of the proclamation of Christ is one of God's great graces for the Church in our day.

Proclamation

There is a clear lesson emerging both from the renewal

movements and from the teaching of recent Vatican documents. It is that the key to evangelisation is proclamation: 'Proclamation is the permanent priority of mission' (Pope John Paul II).[9] The apostles were commanded to 'go out into all the world and preach the gospel to the whole creation' (Mark 16:15). Preach, announce, proclaim, bear witness - these are all English translations of the various Greek words to speak forth the good news.

We do not bring people to faith by teaching them the whole Catechism, ancient or modern. We do not bring them to faith by argumentation or explanation. The Church is like a house that contains great treasures. But the treasures can only be enjoyed through entering the house, and the house can only be entered through the door. The door is the gospel, the good news of salvation. As we have seen, this is not primarily the imparting of doctrine and theology, but the proclamation of an event. This proclamation of the death and resurrection of Jesus was originally known as the *kerygma*,[10] the message announced by the herald, the *kerux*. It is this message that pierces the heart and elicits faith. Only when this has happened is a person ready to enter the catechumenate, to learn more about Christ and to be prepared for baptism.

Proclamation produces faith and builds faith.[11] Why? First, because our Christian heritage as sons and daughters of the Father is the fruit of these saving events. We have to accept these events in order to enter into their fruit. Secondly, because the proclamation is an expression of the deep personal conviction of the herald; the one who proclaims is certain of these events and has staked his or her life on them. The depth of personal conviction that carries the certainty of faith is central to the impact of proclamation.

Correcting two mistakes

There are two mistaken policies that the new emphasis on proclamation corrects. The first is the idea that the Catholic faith is effectively communicated by presenting the whole of divine revelation at every stage. This approach has characterised much of our religious education in Catholic schools from primary through to secondary level. It is as though we give a four-course meal with all the trimmings to everyone in the family including the babies and small children. The result of this policy is that many church-going Catholics have been initiated into a religious system without being led to a personal encounter with the Lord. They have been what the late Cardinal Suenens described as 'sacramentalised' but not evangelised. This does not mean, as some unsympathetic Protestants would say, that these people know nothing about God, and have never received anything authentic from God. But it does mean that they have not been effectively initiated into the heart of the Christian faith and the privileges of the new covenant: an intimacy of relationship with Jesus Christ, the indwelling, guidance and empowering of the Holy Spirit, knowing the all-encompassing love of the heavenly Father. Their situation can perhaps be compared with someone eeking out an existence in a garden shed without knowing they have been invited into the nearby mansion.

I am not saying there is no place for the religious education of children. I have little pastoral experience of the Christian formation of children. But I suspect that where this education has borne fruit, it has been because there has been some form of proclamation, probably within the home. What I am saying, therefore, is that without proclamation, there will be little conversion. And without conversion, schematic education will not produce living faith. Christian initiation, initiation into the Church's worship, initiation into sacramental communion, requires proclamation and conversion.

The second mistake that clear proclamation corrects is the idea that explanation of Catholic doctrine is sufficient to bring people to faith. The old-fashioned apologetics that aimed to demolish by argument all the positions of Protestants and atheists cannot of its nature produce faith. It is true that reason and argument can remove obstacles to faith, but the gift of God that is apt to produce faith is the gift of the word - of the word proclaimed.

We need to be careful that we do not replace proclamation with explanation. Living proclamation requires personal conviction in the speaker in a way that theological or liturgical explanation does not. There is a place for explanation, but it should be subservient to the proclamation of God's Word. The difference can be seen from the Constitution on the Liturgy's description of the different roles of the homilist, whose responsibility is 'the proclamation of God's wonderful works in the history of salvation'[12], and of a commentator, whose role is more explanatory.[13]

To conclude, then, the Holy Spirit is making the Church more evangelistic. We are probably only at an early stage in this process of rediscovery. Because of the radical character of what the Church is rediscovering, and the Church's reluctance to abandon long-standing and well-tried practices, we are at a stage where the need for proclamation is being recognised, but the implications for Catholic practice, including religious education, are not yet clear. We should expect further development in our understanding as Catholic proclamation of the gospel increases and as it produces more fruit throughout the world.

Chapter Three

The Holy Spirit makes the Church more Evangelistic

II: What can/should we learn from the Evangelicals?

The last chapter on how the Holy Spirit has been making the Catholic Church more evangelistic left out one very significant dimension. It said nothing about ecumenism, and the contribution of other Christians to this aspect of Catholic renewal. There are at least two major reasons why this lack needs to be rectified. First, in our day when the Holy Spirit has been constantly bringing the ecumenical issue to the fore,[1] it would be sinning against the Holy Spirit to imagine that the Catholic Church can be renewed in this or any other area completely on its own, without the contribution of other Christian traditions. Secondly, the Catholic rediscovery of direct proclamation of the gospel has in fact been taking place with significant input from other Christians, particularly the Evangelicals and the Pentecostals, for whom evangelism has always been a priority. World-wide, it is the Evangelical and Pentecostal Churches that have been growing the fastest. They are therefore the other Christians from whom we should expect to learn most about how to evangelise and preach the gospel.

Pioneering initiatives

It was a realisation of these evangelical skills in evangelism and of Catholic weakness in this area that led a remarkable Polish priest back in the 1970s, Fr Franciszek Blachnicki, to take a bold initiative. Fr Blachnicki had a remarkable story. As a young man during the war, he had been imprisoned and condemned to death but, most unusually with the Nazis, he was reprieved. He had promised the Lord that if he was spared, he would live his life in God's service, so after the war he offered himself for the priesthood and was ordained. In his desire to spread the gospel at a time when Catholic youth organisations in Poland were forbidden by the Communist government, Fr Blachnicki organised retreats for altar boys. As the altar boys got older, they wanted to receive further formation from Fr Blachnicki. This was the origin of the Oasis movement - renamed Light-Life in 1976 - that was the spiritual backbone of the Solidarity trade union movement and a major cause of the non-violence of Solidarity.

Fr Blachnicki was aware that evangelical groups had success in their evangelism, and that they had expertise in evangelistic training. He felt strongly that the Catholic opening to other Christians at Vatican II required a working together in evangelisation. In fact, by the 1970s he was convinced that the lack of dynamism in the ecumenical movement was because Catholics and Protestants did not preach the gospel together. So Fr Blachnicki asked the Protestant parachurch movement, Campus Crusade for Christ, if they would teach the young Catholics in Oasis how to evangelise and win converts to Christ. His only condition, which they accepted, was that they would respect the Catholic faith of these young Poles, and not seek to separate them from the Catholic Church. This help from Campus Crusade imparted to Light-Life a new evangelistic thrust that contributed to increased growth.[2]

Another pioneering work developed out of their experience in Poland in the form of Youth with a Mission (YWAM). Like Campus Crusade, YWAM was an evangelical-style para-church movement with a major focus on evangelism and discipling. Unlike Campus Crusade, YWAM was overtly charismatic. Their national director in Austria, Bruce Clewett, began to question in his mind the wisdom and the propriety of encouraging young Poles, brought to conversion through YWAM evangelism, to leave the Catholic Church. He saw that this was uprooting them from their culture and their history. Out of this reflection came a long process of asking himself whether he could in conscience work to renew and build up the Catholic Church. Clewett formulated this question in characteristically Evangelical terms: 'Can a Bible-believing Christian in conscience encourage young Catholics to remain in an unbiblical Church?'

After two years of wrestling with this question, Clewett came to a clarity that it was not only wise to do this, but right. His interior struggle had led Clewett to study Catholic teaching and to become acquainted with the documents and the decisions of Vatican II. It then took him some six years to win the approval of the international YWAM leadership for this policy: to devote

YWAM resources, particularly of personnel, specifically to the evangelisation and training of young Catholics in order to serve the renewal of the Catholic Church. Austria and Ireland were the first countries in which YWAM developed this new strategy, which has since been followed through in some other places, in particular in Uganda. Out of YWAM's Catholic apostolate has come a new grouping of communities called RELaY,[3] which is mostly made up of those Catholic communities that have a strong evangelistic thrust and that have been most helped by YWAM.

In fact, one of the major new evangelistic initiatives in the Catholic Church, the International Catholic Program for Evangelisation (ICPE), founded in Malta in 1985, was largely inspired by YWAM. In its origins, ICPE sought to learn from the YWAM discipleship training schools and to adapt their formation methods in evangelisation and discipleship to a Catholic context. YWAM leaders like Clewett encouraged this development, and lent their help to get ICPE off the ground. ICPE now has schools for the formation of Catholic evangelists in Malta, Germany and New Zealand.

The sharpness of the message

What is it that Fr Blachnicki saw in Campus Crusade and that RELaY and ICPE have received from YWAM? Perhaps it can be put best like this: the Evangelicals are like archers with one brand of arrow in their quivers. The gospel message in their mouths is like an arrow with a sharp point that is aimed at a definite target. This message is received when the arrow of the gospel pierces a receptive heart - there is a sharpness to the message, and its aim is to pierce the heart. We should therefore look for the strength of evangelical and pentecostal evangelistic work primarily in the sharpness of their message, rather than their technique or style.

The Evangelicals have focused on the good news of the gospel, especially the proclamation of the saving death of Jesus. They preach the core message that Paul delivered to the Corinthians: 'For I delivered to you as of first importance what I also received, that Christ died for our sins in accordance with the scriptures, that he was buried, that he was raised on the third day... and that he appeared to Cephas, then to the twelve' (1 Cor. 15:3-5). Jesus has done something for us that we could not do for ourselves. To enter into this new life, and to be freed from the power of sin and death, we need to recognise our need, to confess our sin, and to receive by faith what Jesus has won for us, who 'was put to death for our trespasses and raised for our justification' (Rom. 4:25).

The impact of Alpha

More recently, there has been a much bigger Catholic opening to Evangelical gifts of evangelism through Catholic use of the Alpha course. Over the last seven years, the Alpha course, pioneered by Sandy Millar and Nicky Gumbel in the Anglican parish of Holy Trinity, Brompton in London,[4] has spread across the world in a most amazing way. In Britain today, there is hardly any town without an Alpha course. It is being used by an extraordinary range of churches and fellowships from Catholic to Pentecostal and 'new church' charismatic. The National Service Committee for the Catholic

Charismatic Renewal in England and Wales established an office to encourage the use of Alpha among Catholics, and within a short time this office was helping Catholics in other countries to promote the use of Alpha among their people.

Why has Alpha had such a remarkable impact? There is a tendency in our technological age to seek the cause of success of any product in its packaging and in the marketing skills of its promoters. In the age of spin doctors, we can attribute Alpha's success to religious spin. It is true that a great deal of careful thought and detailed preparation has gone into the publication and promotion of the Alpha course. Holy Trinity, Brompton had been running an Alpha course for many years for themselves before it was marketed for export. It is also true that the Alpha course has been designed to impact the non-churchgoer, the person who knows nothing about Christianity, and who regards church as boring and irrelevant. Much effort went into making the presentations attractive and understandable to people outside the Church. It is also true that Alpha emphasises participation and fellowship. The course includes simple meals together each week, and a group weekend away. The format encourages people to express their views without instant correction from a leader.

However, the success of Alpha is not simply of people persevering through the fifteen sessions, and of finding them interesting, but of real conversions resulting in impressive testimonies. This cannot just be the result of technique and social organisation. It comes from proclamation of the gospel, leading to the invitation to faith and conversion. The success of Alpha is the result of the core gospel message being expressed in a language that non-churchgoers can understand and with a freshness that dispels their false stereotypes of Christianity.

Thus the opening talk in Alpha presents Christian faith as 'living life to the full'.[5] The next two talks address 'Who is Jesus?' and 'Why did Jesus die?'. The effects of sin, not often addressed in contemporary Catholic material, are clearly presented in a context that affirms the victory of the cross and the resurrection. We find in Alpha another Evangelical strength, an ability to be practical. Specific talks address the questions: 'Why and how should I read the Bible?', 'Why and how do I pray?', 'How can I be filled with the Spirit?' and 'How can I resist evil?'.

From what has been said about RCIA, it will be seen that Alpha largely corresponds to the primary or initial proclamation. It is not a substitute for catechesis. A big plus for Catholic parishes using Alpha is that it involves a mobilisation of the people to reach their friends and acquaintances, who do not go to church and often have no links at all with any church. This addresses one of our weaknesses, for those entering RCIA have generally come to the Church/clergy, rather than the Church/people going to them. When people enrol for RCIA after doing Alpha, they are coming because they have experienced an initial conversion, and so they are ready for the catechesis that RCIA has to offer. By contrast, many of those who now come to RCIA really need the pre-catechumenate to bring them to initial conversion, but often they have been taken straight into catechesis without adequate concern for this foundational conversion of heart.

Discontinuity and continuity

Catholics often balk at this 'Evangelical gospel'. Perhaps we do not like the language of substitution, of Jesus taking our place and bearing our sin. Perhaps we think that any idea of punishment for sin is incompatible with a loving God. We may prefer to emphasise the solidarity of Jesus with all human suffering and the Father's love for all shown through Jesus Christ. But this smacks too much of the attitudes of pre-ecumenical days when one group of Christians opposed one part of God's revelation emphasised by their religious rivals.

In fact, Catholic-Evangelical interaction is still much influenced and shaped by this kind of opposition. Learning from Evangelicals how to evangelise means discovering where their emphases are complementary, not simply opposed, to ours as Catholics. The key issue here is the relationship between discontinuity and continuity in God's dealings with the human race. Evangelical Protestants have emphasised the discontinuity in God's dealings with humanity. They emphasise God's intervention, and its immediate character. They look for God to act directly from heaven without human mediation: they see conversion as a new birth that is the direct work of God; they see revival as the Spirit of God falling upon the masses. While looking for mass conversions in revival, Evangelicals typically focus on the individual; they are suspicious of tradition, and of any idea of human mediation.

By contrast, Catholics emphasise the continuity in God's dealings with the human race. The Catholic focus is on the Church, coming down through history since the time of the apostles. God's grace and salvation are seen as mediated through the Church, through liturgy, through sacraments, through the ordained ministry. The individual is blessed through the Church and in the Church. Thus Catholics think more corporately and are less focused on the response of each individual. Because the Church is in process through history, Catholics typically see conversion and salvation as process, blessings that continue and grow throughout our lives. The idea of sudden intervention by the Lord easily appears alien, or at least abnormal.[6]

However, closer examination should show us that the biblical story of salvation involves both discontinuity and continuity, both sovereign actions of the Lord and historical process. It is false and confusing to oppose them, and to suggest that God's work of salvation is all one or all the other. The supreme example is the incarnation. The Son of God taking on a human nature, the Word becoming flesh, is totally divine intervention: but this act of God involves an entry into human history and requires the faith-consent of Mary. So there is immediate divine action, leading to the human involvement of Mary and the human history of Jesus. We express this twofold aspect in the Creed: 'He was conceived by the Holy Spirit, and was born of the Virgin Mary.' Jesus is conceived through the immediate action of God (the element of discontinuity), and enters the process of human formation, initially within the womb of his mother (the element of continuity).

The discontinuity-continuity pattern is repeated in the death and resurrection of Jesus. This is of supreme importance for our theme because the 'Passover of Jesus' is the cause of our salvation. Our salvation comes about through faith and baptism ('He who believes and is baptised will be saved,' Mark 16:16), baptism into the death of Jesus (Rom. 6:3-4). But death and resurrection is not a continuous process. Death has its own finality. Resurrection is a sovereign intervention of the Lord. It is not just a reversal of death, but a new creative act of God that produces a qualitatively different life, the life of glory. 'For we know that Christ being raised from the dead will never die again; death no longer has dominion over him' (Rom. 6:9).

Paul makes it very clear that death-resurrection is the pattern for conversion that is symbolised in baptism. The initial coming to faith of the Christian is necessarily an intervention of the Holy Spirit. We cannot produce faith any more than we can produce resurrection. 'But to all who received him, who believed in his name, he gave power to become children of God; who were born, not of blood nor of the will of the flesh nor of the will of man, but of God' (John 1:12-13). Thus it is by the preaching of the discontinuity of the resurrection that the Holy Spirit produces the discontinuity of conversion. There is an element of continuity in that it is the same person who dies and is raised, the same person who is converted from one lifestyle to another. But what is crucial in each case is the action of God.

It is only when the sovereign actions of God in incarnation, resurrection and second coming are clearly preached that clear-cut conversions will follow. If we present entry into the Christian life as simply process, as improvement, as progress, but not as re-birth to new life, not as new creation, then we will not be promoting authentic conversions. This is the heart of the challenge of the Evangelicals and the Pentecostals to the Catholic Church with regard to evangelisation. As we receive their witness concerning God's action in rebirth and conversion, we will be recovering a fully biblical understanding of God's action in discontinuity and continuity, in divine intervention and human response.

God's action and the sacraments

This challenge from the Evangelicals and Pentecostals has major implications for Catholic understanding and practice of the sacraments. For in the typical Catholic-Evangelical contrast, the sacraments exemplify Catholic continuity, together with the mediating role of the Church and her ordained ministry. Evangelical emphasis on discontinuity and divine intervention is exemplified in their opposition to any idea that sacraments cause grace, and their insistence on the immediate action of the Holy Spirit.

At first sight, it might appear that Catholic sacramental practice is all based on the principle of historical continuity and mediation, and that Evangelical-Pentecostal practice is all based on the principle of God's immediate action expressed through historical discontinuity. So, Catholic sacramental celebrations follow a pattern passed down through Christian history; they are structured activities of the Church, with set liturgies and rubrics, led by the ordained ministry. By contrast,

Evangelicals and Pentecostals typically avoid any appearance of ritual, emphasising the freedom of the preacher to preach the word of God and the sovereignty of God who alone can act upon the inner person and bring about the 'miracle' of rebirth. It is God alone who can act upon a mass of people and bring about revival.[7]

However, the sacraments are, according to Catholic faith, celebrations of the paschal mystery of Jesus Christ. As the Catechism states: 'Christian liturgy not only recalls the events that saved us but actualises them, makes them present. The Paschal mystery of Christ is celebrated, not repeated. It is the celebrations that are repeated, and in each celebration there is an outpouring of the Holy Spirit that makes the unique mystery present' (para. 1104).

In other words, each sacramental celebration is a commemoration in the power of the Holy Spirit of the unique event of our salvation, which expresses the discontinuity and the immediacy of God's action in the incarnation and in the resurrection of Jesus Christ. This is as true of the sacraments that can be repeated, like the eucharist, as of those that cannot, like baptism. In baptism, we are marked with the unique event of Christ's death and resurrection, while in the eucharist, we share in and feed on this same unique event.

The challenge for Catholic people, priests and laity, is to rediscover the action of the Holy Spirit in all Christian life and particularly in the liturgy. We have to be freed from all attitudes and mentalities that consider the liturgy and the sacraments as the property of the Church, and under the Church's control, as though the Church controls the Holy Spirit and organises things for God. It is true that the liturgy is a precious heritage received from the past, and that it is not for individuals to adopt a pick-and-choose attitude to this heritage. We respect the heritage because the liturgy belongs to God and is the work of Christ in the Holy Spirit. We are called, then, to celebrate the liturgy as a community living by the Holy Spirit. Bishops and priests do have a responsibility for right order in the liturgy, but we must distinguish responsibility from control. Responsibility recognises the Lordship of the Holy Spirit, whereas control does not.

In particular, this means preaching what we commemorate and celebrate: the Paschal mystery of Christ in all its uniqueness, in its total divine origination, with the human discontinuity of incarnation and resurrection within the continuity of God's unchanging will and the history of salvation. We have to preach that Jesus our Lord 'was put to death for our trespasses and raised for our justification' (Rom. 4:25). We have to preach that baptism is a decisive break and a new creation. Living the baptismal reality of Christ, we continue to feed on the mystery of the eucharist throughout our Christian lives. There is a direct link between an evangelical preaching of the gospel and the sacramental commemoration of the mystery of Christ in its God-given uniqueness.

Just as there is an Evangelical challenge to the Catholic Church to rediscover the discontinuity of God's immediate action within the mediation of Church and liturgy, so there is a Catholic challenge to the Evangelicals and Pentecostals to discover the elements of mediation and of historical continuity. It is not my purpose to develop this point here, as this book is primarily directed to Catholics. But it should not be too difficult for those who are open to such a mutual learning to see that the conversion patterns in Evangelical circles are not without human mediation and continuity. Evangelism and witnessing are themselves forms of mediating salvation, and there is what we might call a divine-human continuity in the gift and the use of the Bible as the word of God.

The need for discernment

How to receive Evangelical strengths into Catholic life inevitably raises the question of how not to receive their weaknesses at the same time. How do we combine these Evangelical strengths with Catholic convictions? This is a challenge for all Catholics seeking to learn how to evangelise. It is a challenge for all Catholic groups using the Alpha course, and for all those engaged in producing post-Alpha materials for Catholic use.

First of all, as long as the liturgy is at the centre of Catholic life, we should not worry about Alpha making the Catholic Church too Protestant. The historical anchoredness of the liturgy provides the Catholic framework in which to revive the truth about the discontinuity of divine intervention. More biblical preaching, especially in liturgical homilies, will deepen the faith of Catholics in the word of God, and help to remove any one-sided emphasis on either word or sacrament.

In this process of learning, discernment will always be needed. Fear does not aid discernment but impedes it. It is important for Catholics to be on their guard against a judgemental attitude that looks down upon and dismisses as worthless the faith and practice of those who are not evidently 'born again' according to Evangelical criteria. The Holy Spirit is at work long before we see the visible signs of God's presence, long before the zealous evangelist appears on the scene, long before we feel the moving of the Spirit for the first time, long before we give a public testimony.

An openness to learn from Evangelicals and Pentecostals will hasten the process of the Catholic Church becoming more evangelistic. Where this learning involves receiving from their strengths, and integrating these with a Catholic understanding of creation and redemption and the Catholic liturgical framework, it will not lead to a dilution or contamination of the Catholic faith, as some Catholics fear. It will lead to mutual enrichment. As we learn from their strengths, the Catholic community will grow in evangelistic power, and as they receive from our strengths, the Evangelicals and Pentecostals will learn more about deeper spiritual formation, and what enables revival impulses to take root and produce lasting fruit. A Catholic Church which becomes more truly evangelistic has an immense potential for ecumenical rapprochement.

Chapter Four

The Holy Spirit makes the Church more Eucharistic

I: Becoming the Church

We might wonder how the Holy Spirit can make the Catholic Church more eucharistic since the Church has always been strongly eucharistic. The eucharist has always been at the heart of Catholic worship. In recent centuries increased devotion has been given to the reserved eucharistic host, which we call the Blessed Sacrament. While it is easy enough to understand that the Holy Spirit is making the Church more evangelistic, how can we say that the Spirit is making the Church more eucharistic?

The eucharist as the gospel enfleshed

In fact, the Holy Spirit making the Church more eucharistic follows directly from the Holy Spirit making the Church more evangelistic. For the eucharist is the gospel enacted. After the proclamation of the death and resurrection of Jesus in the liturgy of the word, we commemorate his death and resurrection in the power of the Spirit. We proclaim, and then we celebrate. In the eucharist, God gives us the reality that we preach.

In this way, the clarity that the Holy Spirit gives us about the core of the gospel leads us to clarity about the heart of our worship. 'In the blessed Eucharist is contained the whole spiritual good of the Church, namely Christ himself, our Pasch' (CCC, para. 1324). The Holy Spirit bringing the word of God to life leads to the Holy Spirit bringing alive the bread of God.[1] Both the word of God and the bread of God, the bread of life, are ultimately the person of Jesus himself.

It is important that our worship consist not only of words but also action. Only as our words of faith are translated into actions of faith do they engage the whole human person. We worship God with our whole beings, with our minds, our hearts and our bodies. So the proclamation of the word and the worship of our lips moves into the sacramental enactment of the sacrifice of Jesus, and our full reception of the word in his total human self-giving. That is to say, the active participation of the Christian people in the liturgy is not just the saying or singing of words, but an entering into the most profound symbolic actions of Christ himself. In the eucharist, we receive and enter into his self-offering to the Father, first in saying Amen to the eucharistic prayer that makes this sacrifice present, and then by receiving his body and blood in communion. This is how the Holy Spirit forms the Christian people into the likeness of Christ. This correlation between word and eucharist, between message and action, then becomes the model for all Christian living. Faith, first confessed in words, must then be manifested in action.

The fullest expression of the Church

Maybe the deepest way in which the Holy Spirit is making the Church more eucharistic concerns the way in which we understand and live the reality of Church. For many centuries, the emphasis in Catholic teaching on the Church was that the Catholic Church is the divinely founded institution or society that mediates God's revelation and salvation to all peoples. Within this picture, the mass was the greatest treasure of the Church. The mass was the most important action that the Church performed. But we did not see so clearly the relationship between the Church and the mass.

The renewal of biblical theology and the renewal of the liturgy in the last fifty to seventy years have led to a new clarity on this relationship. The mass is not just something, even the most important thing, that the Church believes in and promotes. The mass or the eucharist is the self-expression of the Church. It is the Church acting out her deepest reality as the people of God, the body of Christ and the temple of the Holy Spirit. This is how Vatican II presents the liturgy: 'The liturgy is the summit towards which the activity of the Church is directed'[2]; 'liturgical services pertain to the whole body of the Church. They manifest it, and have effects upon it.'[3]

In the celebration of the mass the Holy Spirit leads us to experience ourselves as Church, gathered together as active members of the Church. The Church is constituted by the presence of Christ in the Spirit: each member is most fully Christian where the presence of Christ is fullest. It is in the liturgy that Jesus Christ is present in the fullest way: he is present in the minister, in the eucharistic action and the eucharistic species (in his body and blood), in his word, in the gathered faithful, especially in the prayer and the singing.[4] It is here that we are most fully members of the Church that is Catholic, addressing the Father through and in his Son in the power of the Holy Spirit, listening to the word of God and being bonded together in agape-communion.[5]

Forming the body of Christ

The Holy Spirit is making the Church more eucharistic through making the Church more consciously the body of Christ. It is impossible to have a proper sense of the Church as the body of Christ apart from the Holy Spirit. It is the Spirit of God that creates the bonds between believers in Christ, and the Spirit does this above all through the eucharist. Is this not what St Paul told the Corinthians: 'Because there is one bread, we who are many are one body, for we all partake of the one bread' (1 Cor. 10:17)? It was probably from the experience of the eucharist, of all feeding on the same body of the Lord, that Paul came to describe the Church as the body of Christ. There seems to be a straight line from 1 Corinthians 10, 'we who are many are one body' (v.17) to 1 Corinthians 12, 'For just as the body is one and has many members, and all the members of the body, though many, are one body, so it is with Christ' (v.12).

By feeding on the body and blood of the Lord, Christians are built up into Christ to form one body in him. 'Grant that we, who are nourished by his body and blood, may be filled with his Holy Spirit, and become one body, one spirit in Christ.'[6] Hence the Church teaches that 'the

Eucharist makes the Church'.[7] Being formed into the body of Christ means being conformed to Christ. It means being filled with the Spirit that filled Jesus; it means taking on the mind of Jesus;[8] it means acquiring the heart of Jesus.

Conformed to Christ

Every Christian is conformed to Christ as they feed on Christ and live by his Spirit. However, there is a particular way in which the ordained ministers of the Church are called to be conformed to Christ. In the eucharist, the minister is called to the deepest identification with Christ to the extent of saying the very words of Jesus, as he holds the bread in his hands: 'This is my body given for you' and as he holds the chalice: 'This is the cup of my blood, the blood of the new and everlasting covenant.'

Becoming more eucharistic has, then, this key dimension of being conformed to Christ. For his ministers, it means becoming more like Jesus in his ministry. In his ministry, Jesus taught and served. Of course there were multiple dimensions to his teaching: evangelistic, apocalyptic, prophetic, didactic. And there were multiple aspects to his service: leading, caring, exorcising, healing. In fact, these two overarching forms of ministry, the teaching and the serving, correspond to the two parts of the liturgy, the liturgy of the word and the liturgy of the sacrament. Every detail in this conformation to Christ the teacher and Christ the servant is the work of the Holy Spirit.

What does it mean to be more like Christ the teacher?

Ordination is to be granted a share in the ministry of Christ. This includes a share in Christ's teaching ministry. The Holy Spirit conforms ordained ministers to Jesus the rabbi-teacher. As the Holy Spirit renews the Church, the Spirit raises up teaching ministries and gives the desire for teaching. In movements of spiritual renewal, the Holy Spirit raises up ministers with gifts of teaching and creates the thirst for teaching among the people. The rise of Catholic charismatic renewal quickly gave rise to a vast number of teaching ministries, and to a great demand for teaching. These two are related. Taste creates a desire for food. Taste of the Holy Spirit creates a desire for the food of spiritual teaching. At the same time, the Holy Spirit raises up multiple gifts of teaching within the body of Christ.[9]

This teaching is not the teaching of theology in the way that we have known either in seminaries or at universities. Neither is it evangelistic preaching aimed at bringing people to conversion. It is more like the instruction we find in the New Testament epistles, especially the pastoral epistles of Paul to Timothy and Titus: that is to say, it is pastoral-practical teaching for believers aimed at a deeper following of the Lord. It is an exposition of the word of God, but not of an academic kind: it is not discussing authorship and textual criticism, but teaching how to live as a Christian and how to lead others in the Christian community. This teaching is accompanied by a concern to identify and to train future leaders.

I believe that in this renewal of the Church the Holy Spirit is making ministers of the word real teachers according to the pattern of Jesus. We can see the emergence of strong bishop-teachers in some places in the Church: most obviously in Pope John Paul II, but also in men like Cardinal Martini of Milan, Cardinal Lustiger of Paris and Cardinal Danneels of Malines-Brussels. They are forming the Church of the future. As bishop-teachers, they are more like the Fathers of the Church than either bishop-administrators or scholar-theologians. This kind of teaching is formative, forming young minds, producing informed disciples, shaping community and developing Christian values that are counter-cultural. The enormous influence of Karol Wojtyla in Poland, even before being elected Pope, illustrates how he understood from the beginning of his priesthood the need to be a teacher-master forming disciples for the Lord.

If we look carefully at the epistles to Timothy and Titus, we will find many references to teaching and training.[10] This teaching-training is directly related to godliness: 'For physical training is of some value, but godliness has value for all things, holding promise for both the present life and the life to come' (1 Tim. 4:8). Paul is a servant and apostle for 'the knowledge of the truth that leads to godliness' (Tit. 1:1). The letter to the Hebrews likens teaching for spiritual infants to milk, and teaching for the mature to solid food (Heb. 5:12-14). That for the mature is described as 'the teaching about righteousness' (5:13). The teaching about righteousness is not simply what we would call moral teaching, but it is living in conformity to Christ Jesus in trinitarian communion. The wording in 1 Timothy 3 is significant:

'the mystery of godliness is great.' What is this mystery? It is the whole programme of the incarnation: 'He appeared in a body, was vindicated by the Spirit, was seen by angels, was preached among the nations, was believed in throughout the world, was taken up in glory' (1 Tim. 3:16). The context shows how Paul held doctrine and morality together: he moves from conduct in God's household, the Church (v. 15), to the mystery of godliness (v.16).

This kind of teaching is a vital necessity. There are more and more people in our parishes who are experiencing or have experienced new life through Life in the Spirit seminars, through Alpha courses, through the Renew programme, through their own reading of the Bible. Many then experience great frustration when they do not find in their parishes the teaching they crave. I have come across quite a number of Catholics who go to mass to receive the eucharist, but also go to new charismatic, Baptist or Anglican Churches for practical biblical teaching. Many so value the eucharist that they would be very hesitant to leave the Catholic Church, but they know that they also need discipleship teaching. Others who have never come to a love of the eucharist simply leave the Church for places where they find food that satisfies them. There is more discipleship teaching in the Protestant sector of the charismatic movement, probably because Protestant teachers come from backgrounds with a stronger grounding in the Bible - it is impossible for strong teaching ministries to develop without a deep knowledge of the scriptures.

I believe that the Holy Spirit wants to make all priests and deacons real teachers in the Church. I am not suggesting that many of us are likely to become Martinis or Lustigers. But at our own level, developing from where we are, in a small way that will grow, I believe that this is possible. How can this be done? Look first at your teaching-preaching opportunities, especially with those who are open to the faith. Think of maybe giving a 5-minute homily at weekday mass. Think of house masses, meetings of parish sodalities and societies, and forms of follow-up to Alpha courses where Alpha has awakened an interest.

This kind of teaching requires planning. People need to be given a vision. Over time, different areas, different moods and rhythms of our lives need to be covered. The church year and the lives of different saints lend themselves to this. Think big, and the Spirit will fill your sails. Such teaching needs to address godliness-righteousness in Christ, how the Spirit conforms us to Jesus in life, in prayer, in service and in ministry. It is the stage at which biblical teaching on Mary is particularly appropriate. It needs to address spiritual battle, intercession, deliverance. But the Catholic framework for mystagogy is that of the mysteries, the sacraments, where we are formed in the life that is hidden with Christ in God, awaiting the day of manifestation, the day of Christ Jesus.

What does it mean to be more like Christ the servant?

There are perhaps two main dimensions to this: first, what kind of activities will we be led into? And secondly, what kind of character will we develop? The first activities that we find in the ministry of Jesus are healings and exorcisms. We see from the beginning of his public ministry the encounter of Jesus with the forces of evil and the consequences of sin. This encounter is presented as a direct consequence of the anointing of Jesus with the Holy Spirit at his baptism in the Jordan. The ministerial activity of Jesus is marked by the exercise of his messianic authority over evil and sin, and the manifestation of his compassion for suffering humanity.

The ordained ministry of the Church is a sharing in the ministry of Jesus Christ. As the Holy Spirit renews our ministry, we will experience afresh the power of the Spirit to bring healing and deliverance to wounded and oppressed humanity, and to express the love of the Lord for the poor and the afflicted. As with Jesus, we will find that a manifestation of the power of the Holy Spirit, especially in preaching, uncovers the presence and activity of evil.[11] There is much evidence today of the influence of evil spirits and spiritual powers of darkness, not least in the horrendous events in Bosnia, Rwanda and Sierra Leone. But the forces of evil are also at work closer to home: in the embittered conflict in Northern Ireland, where apparent breakthroughs seem to lead to recurring disappointment; in multiple forms of addiction; in moral corruption and unrestrained greed; in the irresponsibility of the arms trade; in the rise of mafia-type crime industries, controlling drugs and pornography; in the spread of spiritualism and the occult. Wherever sin is embraced and becomes a lifestyle, the demonic powers get a foothold and then a grip on societies, groups and persons.

The renewing work of the Spirit will lead the ministers of the Church increasingly into situations of conflict where a prime need is deliverance from spiritual oppression and subjugation. As Cardinal Ratzinger has recognised: 'It is no accident that whereas a reductionist theology treats the devil and the world of evil spirits as a mere label, there is in the "renewal" a new and concrete awareness of the powers of evil, in addition, of course, to the calm certainty of the power of Christ who subjugates them all.'[12] Many people are incapable of turning to God until they are freed from the powers that hold them in bondage.

Our pastoral training and practice still pay insufficient attention to this area as well as the preparation of priests for ministries of healing and deliverance. Very few dioceses seem to have guidelines to priests to encourage them in a ministry for which they may be unaware there is a great need, and to make clear the exceptional cases that need to be referred to the local bishop because of their gravity.[13] This is an area in which the Anglicans have led the way in terms of mature healing ministries and in terms of theologically and psychologically competent reports.[14] One of the best occasions for such healing and deliverance ministry are regular, perhaps monthly, healing masses; these often attract large crowds because the suffering will always seek relief, and they provide an effective instrument for evangelisation and renewal. Personal ministry within the eucharist, for example the laying on of hands after communion, emphasises the healing role of the church community and avoids many of the dangers of ministries that focus on the healing minister and on the 'miraculous'.[15]

The caring dimension to Jesus' ministry was a being

with people in love, a sympathy in the deepest sense of 'suffering with'. 'The Lord is good to all; he has compassion on all he has made... The Lord upholds all those who fall and lifts up all who are bowed down' (Ps. 145:8, 14). As the Spirit conforms us to Christ, we will find a compassionate, caring character develop within us. The compassion of the Lord is supremely expressed in his giving us food: when Jesus saw the crowd, he called the disciples to him and said, 'I have compassion for these people; they have already been with me three days and have nothing to eat' (Matt. 15:32). The Lord's compassion extends to this unimaginable gift: that he feeds us with his own body and blood.

We are ordained to a self-sacrificing ministry. To be conformed to Christ is to be willing to suffer. Jesus himself pointed to the contrast between the Good Shepherd, who lays down his life for his sheep, and the hireling, who flees as soon as the wolf appears (John 10:12). To follow Jesus is to be willing to appear a failure, to face being misunderstood, to be mocked and ridiculed, to stand up to criticism. It is to be a man of principle.

This is perhaps particularly difficult in our society. We live in an age where it is very difficult for public figures to be people of principle. The media will point out every inconsistency: this is what you said on 4th May 1996 and now you say the opposite on 21st September 2000. Opinion polls tell politicians that if they are sympathetic to asylum-seekers they will not get re-elected. Yet we are followers of him who 'endured the cross, scorning its shame' (Heb. 12:2). This line is followed by an exhortation: 'Consider him who endured such opposition from sinful men, so that you will not grow weary and lose heart' (Heb. 12:3).

My remarks on the Christian minister as teacher and servant may seem to have wandered from the theme of the eucharist. But I am saying that the eucharist makes us more like Christ the teacher and Christ the servant, and being more like Christ in teaching and service conforms us more deeply to the eucharistic action. To become more eucharistic is not just to have a deeper appreciation for the mass and a deeper devotion to the Lord in the Blessed Sacrament; it is to be made more like Jesus in the word and in the sacrament. It is to be made self-givers in our words and in our actions. It is to empty ourselves so that we teach Christ and not our ideas; it is to empty ourselves so that we feed people with Christ and not with ourselves. The eucharist is the summit of our ministry: first because here we are most identified with Christ; secondly, because we bring our ministry in all its weakness to this celebration of Jesus and the Church that transcends all our limitations.

The Holy Spirit's work of conforming us to Jesus Christ has both a personal and a corporate character. It is not just the individual bishop, priest or deacon who is being made more like Christ; it is also the Church community that is being made more like him. The Holy Spirit making the Church more eucharistic is then making the Church more like Christ in his passion, death and resurrection. The Church that feeds on the Lamb once slain is being prepared for her own passover into glory: 'The new Passover [of Jesus] is anticipated in the [Last]

Supper and celebrated in the Eucharist, which fulfils the Jewish Passover and anticipates the final Passover of the Church in the glory of the kingdom' (CCC, para. 1340). The Church that is more eucharistic is more deeply prepared for 'this final Passover, when she will follow her Lord in his death and resurrection' (CCC, para. 677) into the fulness of the kingdom ushered in by his second coming.

Chapter Five

The Holy Spirit makes the Church more Eucharistic

II: The Church that remembers

The biblical renewal in the Church has been leading to a new awareness of the importance of remembrance: first in the life of Israel, and then in the life of the Church. This is a vital dimension in the Holy Spirit making the Church more eucharistic.

The Church remembers

In its section on the Holy Spirit in the liturgy, the Catechism makes a most striking statement: 'The Holy Spirit is the Church's living memory' (para. 1099). This phrase links up with the word of Jesus about the Holy Spirit that 'he will take what is mine and declare it to you' (John 16:14). That is to say, the Holy Spirit will always remind the Church of the life, deeds and words of her Lord, and will make these present and efficacious in her midst.

The Holy Spirit is in the business of remembrance. This may surprise those who think that the Holy Spirit is only concerned with the here and now, with vitality now, with immediate spiritual results. But Christian faith is grounded in the history of Israel preparing for the coming in flesh of the Son of God. The Holy Spirit not only bridges the gap between heaven and earth, but also the gap between the time of Jesus and the present day.

One of the most essential tasks of the Church is to remember. All the liturgy involves remembering: the liturgy of the word and the celebration of the sacraments. The Catechism tells us: 'The liturgy is the memorial of the mystery of Christ' (para. 1099). The Holy Spirit is the principal agent of this recalling. The Holy Spirit brings both word and sacrament to life. 'The Holy Spirit first recalls the meaning of the salvation event to the liturgical assembly by giving life to the Word of God' (CCC, para. 1100). It is the word of God that gives birth to faith, and faith is then the life-blood of the sacraments. The remembering in the liturgy of the word leads to the remembering in the sacramental action.

The memorial character of the sacraments is particularly important in relation to the eucharist. In the mass we obey the command of Jesus: 'Do this in remembrance of me' (Luke 22:19; see also 1 Cor. 11:24). The new eucharistic prayers bring out both *anamnesis*, memorial, and *epiclesis*, invocation of the Holy Spirit. As the summit of the Church's worship, the eucharist illustrates memorial and invocation the most strongly. 'Together with the anamnesis, the epiclesis is at the heart of each sacramental celebration, most especially of the Eucharist' (CCC, para. 1106).

Memorial and sacrifice

The theological squabbles over the eucharist after the Protestant Reformation tended to present a straight opposition between sacrifice (Catholic) and memorial (Protestant). Sacrifice meant real presence of the Lord, and memorial meant (for Catholics) real absence. Many Protestants said of the Lord's supper, 'it's a mere memorial', or 'it's only a symbol', using the word symbol in a weak sense. The renewal of biblical studies has made clear that the Christian memorial of the eucharist is based on the Jewish memorial of the Passover. The Jews have a strong conception of memorial: as they celebrate the Passover, the Jews believe that in some way they participate in the event being remembered. In some mysterious way, this event is made present to them. 'This is how Israel understands its liberation from Egypt: every time Passover is celebrated, the Exodus events are made present to the memory of believers so that they may conform their lives to them' (CCC, para. 1363).

In the eucharist, the memorial of Jesus' Passover to the Father is even stronger: it is made in the power of the Holy Spirit. So paragraph 1104 of the Catechism bears repeating: 'Christian liturgy not only recalls the events that saved us but actualises them, makes them present. The Paschal mystery of Christ is celebrated, not repeated. It is the celebrations that are repeated, and in each celebration there is an outpouring of the Holy Spirit that makes the unique mystery present.'

The Church's renewed understanding does not deny that the eucharist is a sacrifice. But it rejects the opposition between sacrifice and memorial. The Catechism teaches: 'Because it is the memorial of Christ's Passover, the eucharist is also a sacrifice' (para. 1365). In the power of the Spirit, the sacrifice of Jesus is recalled and made present, and for this reason the eucharist is a sacrificial action.

A transformation in ministry and worship

The transformation in Catholic worship through the liturgical movement fully endorsed by the Second Vatican Council has involved at its heart a rediscovery of the role of the Holy Spirit in Catholic worship and ministry. Here a lot of important learning was to be had from other Christian traditions, particularly those of the Eastern Church, which has always emphasised the importance of the invocation of the Holy Spirit, the *epiclesis*, in the eucharistic prayers. Worship is only possible through the Holy Spirit. Sanctification is only possible through the Holy Spirit. Renewed liturgy is only possible through a renewed attention to the Holy Spirit.

This transformation is not just a change in theology and in teaching, but a transformation in how to minister, how to lead worship, how to preach. It is to learn a dependence on the Holy Spirit. It is here, perhaps, that we see the most important contribution of the charismatic movement and other currents of spiritual renewal to the celebration of our liturgy. We discover that the liturgical texts and rubrics are a necessary framework, like a human skeleton. But the skeleton needs flesh and blood, needs the breath of life, the Spirit. Here the post-Vatican II reforms have provided a range of new alternatives, especially a choice of eucharistic prayers, together with places where the text is offered as a model that the celebrant can either use or adapt, for example in the introductions to the penitential rite and the Our Father.

Dependence on the Holy Spirit does not mean a lack of human preparation. But it does call for a different *type* of human preparation. In his biography of Pope John Paul II, George Weigel recounts how the Holy Father, throughout his years as archbishop of Krakow and as Pope in Rome, has set aside two hours each morning before the Lord in chapel to write sermons, pastoral letters, encyclicals. The Holy Spirit is always particular: God loves this person, God speaks to us personally, God heals this wound. So the preparation of the Spirit - for preaching, for worship - makes us attentive to the particular will of God for this audience, for this assembly. The Holy Spirit will also influence the way we lead worship. The Spirit will make us attentive to what is happening in the hearts of the people, giving the celebrant a sense of when to pause, when to proceed, when to adapt.

Charismatic renewal and the eucharist

The main thrust of renewal, making the Church more eucharistic, has come from the work of biblical and liturgical scholars and the ministry of pastoral liturgists with their people. Catholic charismatic renewal has illustrated, particularly in France and Italy, a wonderful integration of liturgical structure and spontaneous response to the leading of the Spirit. As the renewal has brought to the fore the diversity of gifts and ministries, so charismatic liturgies have enhanced eucharistic celebrations by offering greater scope for the exercise of this diversity. They have also enhanced the service-role of directors of music in channelling the praise and worship of the people as the Spirit leads.

The charismatic movement has also raised Christian awareness of the heavenly dimension of Christian life and worship. As the Holy Spirit is sent from heaven, so the gift of the Holy Spirit brings us a share in the heavenly life of Christ. So St Paul tells the Philippians that 'our commonwealth is in heaven' (Phil. 3:20). To the Ephesians, he writes that God has 'made us alive together with Christ... and raised us up with him, and made us sit with him in the heavenly places in Christ Jesus' (Eph. 2:5-6). That is why he tells the Colossians: 'For you have died, and your life is hid with Christ in God' (Col. 3:3).

Since it is only the Holy Spirit that can make the Church conscious of her heavenly character, it is only the Holy Spirit who can restore to the Church a full consciousness of the heavenly dimension of the eucharist. This consciousness has been strongest in the Eastern Church, that always retained a sense of the eucharistic action on earth as a participation in the eternal liturgy of heaven. This conviction also found expression in the teaching of Vatican II: 'In the earthly liturgy we share in a foretaste of that heavenly liturgy which is celebrated in the Holy City of Jerusalem towards which we journey as pilgrims, where Christ is sitting at the right hand of God, minister of the sanctuary and of the true tabernacle.'[1] In the Catholic mass of the Roman rite, this earthly-heavenly relationship is expressed most clearly at the end of the preface, where the preface leads into the Holy, Holy, Holy, with words such as, 'Now, with angels and archangels, and the whole company of heaven, we sing the unending hymn of your praise'.[2] Eucharistic Prayer I, the Roman Canon, also refers to the heavenly worship: 'Almighty God, we pray that your angel may take this sacrifice to your altar in heaven.'

The high priesthood of Jesus

The citation above from Vatican II refers to the heavenly ministry of Christ in language taken from the letter to the Hebrews.[3] Another paragraph in the Constitution on the Liturgy had referred to each liturgical celebration being 'an action of Christ the priest and of his body'.[4] The letter to the Hebrews is the only book of the New Testament that develops the idea of Jesus the high priest. This letter also has the most teaching about the heavenly character of the Christian life.[5] We should expect, then, that the Holy Spirit will unfold further from Hebrews the heavenly dimension of Christian worship and particularly of the eucharist. This will be another important way in which the Holy Spirit is making the Church more eucharistic.

In fact, it was an extraordinarily bold move for the Jewish author of Hebrews to give Jesus the title of high priest. For the Jews, it was evident that only the sons of Aaron could become high priest, but Jesus belonged to the tribe of Judah, and was not a descendant of Levi and Aaron. The author deals with this problem by taking up the prophetic promise of Psalm 110: 'You are a priest for ever, after the order of Melchizedek' (Ps. 110:4). Quite a section of Hebrews is taken up with showing the superiority of the high priesthood of Melchizedek to that of

Aaron and his descendants. Abraham paid tithes to Melchizedek, and tithes are only paid to one who is superior.[6] So the author of Hebrews says that the high priesthood of Jesus is superior because it is exercised in heaven, it is eternal, his sacrifice is made once and for all and he is holy and blameless.[7]

We are probably accustomed to thinking that Jesus acted as priest on Calvary in offering his life for all sinners, and that in heaven he acts as Lord rather than as priest. However, what the letter to the Hebrews brings out is that Jesus exercises his high priesthood for ever in heaven: 'We have such a high priest, one who is seated at the right hand of the throne of the Majesty in heaven, a minister in the sanctuary and the true tent which is set up not by man but by the Lord' (Heb. 8:1-2). 'For Christ has entered, not into a sanctuary made with hands, a copy of the true one, but into heaven itself, now to appear in the presence of God on our behalf' (Heb. 9:24).

This vision of Jesus exercising his high priesthood in heaven, following the once-and-for-all sacrificial death on Calvary, does in fact correspond with the Israelite understanding of sacrifice. For, as biblical studies have shown, while the priest had a role in the killing of the sacrificial victim, the essential task of the priest was to take the blood of the victim and to sprinkle it upon the altar. So in the book of Leviticus many instructions are given concerning sacrificial offerings. In several cases, the man bringing the animal kills it; in some cases it is the high priest, as on the day of atonement;[8] but always the pouring of the blood is done by the priests. 'Then he shall kill the bull before the Lord; and Aaron's sons the priests shall present the blood, and throw the blood round about against the altar that is at the door of the tent of meeting' (Lev. 1:5).[9] The sacrifice was the whole action, the killing and the sprinkling of the blood, not just the killing. It is against this background that the author of Hebrews presents the high priestly ministry of Jesus. Jesus exercises his high priesthood in heaven, where he eternally presents his blood that was shed once upon the cross: 'He [Christ] entered once for all into the Holy Place, taking not the blood of goats and calves, but his own blood, thus securing an eternal redemption' (Heb. 9:12).

Jesus the high priest and the eucharist

What bearing does all this have on the eucharist? Can the letter to the Hebrews help both Catholic and Protestant beyond the controversies of the past? At first sight, this may seem unlikely since the letter to the Hebrews has been a major quarry for Protestant arguments against the Catholic teaching that the mass is a sacrifice. For it is this letter that teaches most explicitly the once-and-for-all character of Jesus' sacrificial death: 'Nor was it to offer himself repeatedly, as the high priest enters the Holy Place yearly with blood not his own; for then he would have had to suffer repeatedly since the foundation of the world' (Heb. 9:25-26). But a way forward beyond the controversies of the past that is truly biblical would seem to lie in greater attention to the teaching of Hebrews that Jesus exercises his high-priestly calling in the heavenly sanctuary.

Both Catholic and Protestant are now agreed that Jesus died once and for all upon the cross for our sins.

'The cross is the unique sacrifice of Christ, "the one mediator between God and men" (CCC, 618).'

The disagreements concern the eucharist, whether in any way it is a sacrifice, and the manner of Christ's presence. The teaching of Hebrews that Jesus has an eternal priesthood that he exercises in the heavenly sanctuary opens the door to an understanding of the eucharist as sacrifice through a participation of the Church on earth in the heavenly priesthood of Jesus.

When the Holy Spirit opens up to us the heavenly dimension of Christ, the Church and the Christian life, we can be freed from the limitations of earthly perspectives. When we think of the relationship between the eucharist we now celebrate and the historic events of the Last Supper and Calvary without a real awareness of the heavenly ministry of Jesus, then we easily become trapped in memorial-versus-sacrifice controversies. There is surely a major breakthrough when we see the earthly and the heavenly dimensions together: that on earth Jesus died once and for all for our sins (one death, one act of self-offering, one shedding of blood) and that in heaven the glorified Jesus, the Lamb 'standing as though it had been slain' (Rev. 5:6), forever pleads this one blood-offering before the Father.

The role of Jesus, the high priest, in the heavens brings out the full role of the Holy Spirit. The Holy Spirit is not only the bridge between the present and the past, between our generation and the earthly life of Christ two thousand years ago, but the Holy Spirit is most importantly the bridge between heaven and earth. So, in the eucharist, the issue of 'once-for-all' death and repeated celebrations of the eucharistic sacrifice is not just one of the Holy Spirit making present now what happened once two thousand years ago. It is rather the Holy Spirit making present on earth the eternal action of Jesus Christ in heaven, with the heavenly reality being understood not as simply another phase after Calvary, but as in some way the taking up of Calvary into the eternal presentation of Jesus' blood.

The rediscovery of the heavenly dimension of the eucharist may enable Catholics and Protestants to come to greater agreement about the eucharist. For without a clear awareness of Jesus' eternal priesthood in the heavens, the Catholic teaching that the eucharist is a sacrifice inevitably appeared to Protestants to be a denial of the once-for-all character of the sacrifice of the cross. But without the heavenly dimension, the Protestant affirmation of the completeness of the once-for-all sacrifice of Calvary seemed to Catholics to reduce Christian practice to private interior faith without any corporate introduction of the Church into the paschal mystery of Jesus' death and resurrection.

High priest according to the order of Melchizedek

There is another fascinating aspect of the teaching of Hebrews on the high priesthood of Jesus that has a bearing on the eucharist. It concerns Jesus being a priest according to the order of Melchizedek. As already alluded to, the mention of Melchizedek was made primarily to explain and justify the claim that Jesus, who was not a descendant of Aaron, is truly high priest. The main teaching of Hebrews concerns the eternal character of this priesthood - 'he holds his priesthood permanently, because he continues for ever' (Heb. 7:24) - and the way in which the high-priestly ministry of Jesus perfects the shadowy reality of the Old Testament priesthood of Aaron and his descendants - 'they serve a copy and shadow of the heavenly sanctuary' (Heb. 8:5).

The fascinating element is that all we know of the offering of Melchizedek is that he 'brought out bread and wine' (Gen. 14:18). Is the author of Hebrews in some way linking the heavenly ministry of Jesus according to the order of Melchizedek to the eucharist, in which there is the offering of bread and wine? The letter to the Hebrews does not make this connection. However, the text of Genesis does go straight from he 'brought out bread and wine' to 'he was priest of God Most High' (Gen. 14:18).

The author of Hebrews was a Jewish believer in Jesus. He would have been very aware of the relationship between the Last Supper, the sacrificial death of Jesus and the Passover. This makes it unlikely that he had no idea of any connection with the eucharist in comparing Jesus to Melchizedek. Maybe there is already here that deep reverence for 'the mysteries' as the Christian liturgy came to be called, that caused hesitation in putting into print the deepest mystery of Christian life and worship. We also need this reverence as we consider how the Holy Spirit is making the Church more eucharistic. This reverence involves taking all the data of scripture and the acts of the Lord, recognising how they transcend our categories and our mental capacities, and avoiding the controversies of the past with their cut-and-dried explanations. Yes, there is a connection between Melchizedek and Jesus in the taking of bread and wine, but let us approach the mystery with deep reverence and respect.

Jesus as heavenly intercessor

The rediscovery of the heavenly realm in the Pentecostal and charismatic movements has contributed to an immense increase in intercessory prayer across the world since the mid-1980s. A new awareness of the influence of evil spirits has led to a renewed under-standing of the New Testament texts that speak of the victory of Jesus over the principalities and powers in the heavenly realms.[10]

Jewish thought at the time of Christ was familiar with the idea of different layers in the heavens. Some writ-ers spoke of three layers, others of seven - both sym-bolic numbers. We find this idea in St Paul, when he speaks of 'a man' (himself it would seem), who 'was caught up to the third heaven' (2 Cor. 12:2), where 'he heard things that cannot be told, which man may not utter' (2 Cor. 12:4). It was in this framework of thought that St Paul speaks in Ephesians of 'the spiritual hosts of wickedness in the heavenly places' (Eph. 6:12), when he warns the Church in Ephesus that they need spiritu-al weapons and spiritual armour to fight against these enemies that are more powerful than mere 'flesh and blood'. Here, we must remember that Paul had already in this epistle spoken of the triumph of Jesus' ascension: 'He who descended is he who also ascended far above all the heavens, that he might fill all things' (Eph. 4:10).

In his ascension, then, Christ has overcome all the forces of evil, rising above the evil powers in the heavenly realms. Similar language is used in Hebrews: 'Since then we have a great high priest who has passed through the heavens, Jesus, the Son of God, let us hold fast our confession' (Heb. 4:14); 'For it was fitting that we should have such a high priest, holy, blameless, unstained, separated from sinners, exalted above the heavens' (Heb. 7:26).

Greater awareness of the powers of darkness leads to greater intensity of intercession. It leads to a clearer sense that intercession involves spiritual warfare. The Holy Spirit strengthens our awareness that the Church is in spiritual conflict with evil forces, and the sense of the victorious might of the ascended Christ. The experience of spiritual renewal with its opening up of the heavenly dimension should then encourage the bringing together of the role of Christ, the heavenly high priest, in the eucharist and the invocation of the heavenly victor on the battlefield of intercession. If, as Catholics believe, the liturgy is the summit of the Church's activity and the eucharist is the summit of liturgical worship, then the Church's most powerful prayer for the defeat of evil is the eucharist. Perhaps the Holy Spirit is leading us towards prayers of intercession in the eucharist that will be more consciously a participation in the heavenly intercession of the one high priest and in his victory over all that is evil. Rather than simply detailing the needs of the Church and of the world, and asking for God's help, such prayers would confess the victory of Jesus over all evil and ask for the manifestation of this victory in the areas of need and conflict.

Thus the Holy Spirit making the Church more eucharistic has a heavenly dimension. The Holy Spirit is making the Church more aware of her communion with the Church in glory, more aware that our worship on earth is united to and reflects the worship of heaven, and more aware of the heavenly ministry of Jesus, in particular as the high priest of our confession.

Chapter Six

The Holy Spirit makes the Church more Ecumenical

I: The Holy Spirit and the unity of the Church

Of the four major transformations in the Church that we are considering, the ecumenical transformation is the most obvious. In the course of the twentieth century, the Catholic Church has changed from having a deep-rooted hostility to other Christian churches and communities - then simply seen as schismatic or heretical - to an acceptance of them as Christian bodies of brothers and sisters in Christ. This transformation is one of the remarkable stories of the last century. It could only have happened through the Holy Spirit. It is not a change from being less ecumenical to more ecumenical, but from a refusal of relationships on principle to a deep and irreversible commitment to reconciliation and unity.

The magisterium and the ecumenical movement

We can see the revolution in Catholic thinking by looking at the key dates and events concerning the ecumenical movement and the Catholic Church. The first key date is 1910, the year generally regarded as the foundation of the modern ecumenical movement. The event was an inter-Protestant missionary conference in Edinburgh, at which the disastrous effects of denominational division and rivalry on Christian missionary work were faced and acknowledged. It was seen that rival presentations of the Christian message by competing missionary bodies were a counter-witness to the gospel. While the missionaries taught the native peoples that Jesus Christ, the Son of God, had overcome all sin, hatred and division on the cross of Calvary, and enabled us to love God and to love one another, their attitudes to the missionaries of other churches contradicted their message. Not only was the Catholic Church not represented at Edinburgh in 1910, but with the notable exception of Bishop Bonomelli of Cremona, the Catholic hierarchy were hardly aware of this meeting.

The second key date is 1928, the year of Pope Pius XI's encyclical *Mortalium animos*. This letter was an emphatic rejection of the ecumenical movement, only two years after the death of the Belgian primate, Cardinal Mercier, who had hosted the first ecumenical dialogue with Catholic participation, the Malines conversations held with some Anglican theologians between 1921 and 1925. Incidentally, this Catholic rejection came after the first opening of the Orthodox Churches to the ecumenical movement in 1920.

The third key date is 1949, when the Vatican issued a brief instruction on the ecumenical movement. It came one year after the first Assembly of the World Council of Churches in Amsterdam, in which the Holy See had refused to allow Catholic participation. The instruction of 1949 did two things: it recognised that the growing desire for unity in the ecumenical movement was 'under the inspiration of the Holy Spirit'; secondly, it allowed Catholics to say the Our Father with 'non-Catholics'.[1] Although this document was short and had little immediate effect on Catholic life, in effect it put a time-bomb underneath the Catholic isolation from the ecumenical movement and under the old moral-canonical teaching forbidding worship with non-Catholics (*communicatio in sacris*) as 'intrinsically evil'. If the ecumenical movement represents an impulse of the Holy Spirit, then why should the Catholic Church not participate in it? And if it is permissible to say the Our Father with Protestants, then how can we continue to say that praying with Protestants is intrinsically evil?

The fourth key date is 1964, the year of the Decree on Ecumenism, *Unitatis redintegratio*, of the Second Vatican Council. In this decree, the Catholic Church effected a sea-change in its relations with other Christian churches and communities. It officially accepted the ecumenical movement and committed the Catholic Church to an ecumenical stance. It rejected the previous attitude that only envisaged the possibility of non-Catholics being saved through 'invincible ignorance'. It no longer refused to recognise a positive role for other Christian bodies in the salvation of their members; previously Catholics thought that if Protestants were saved, it was in spite of their church membership, not through it. The decree recognised that 'the separated churches and communities as such... have by no means been deprived of significance and importance in the mystery of salvation.'[2]

How did this revolution come about?

None of the developments and changes in the teaching of the magisterium descend from heaven without earthly preparation. There is invariably a preparation in the spiritual realm, preparation through prayer, and a preparation in the theological realm, through research and re-thinking. There were many ecumenical pioneers in the Catholic Church whom we should honour for their vision, their courage and their perseverance against great odds. One who combined this work of prayer and theology was Dom Lambert Beauduin (1873-1960), who suffered long suspicion and exile for his ecumenical convictions. Beauduin had founded the Belgian Benedictine monastery of Amay, later at Chevetogne, to pray and work for the unity of the divided body of Christ. Two pioneers of major significance, who represented respectively the spiritual and the theological preparation, both came from France: the Abbé Paul Couturier of Lyon (1881-1953), who transformed the annual Week of Prayer for Christian Unity around 1933; and the Dominican theologian, Père Yves Congar (1904-95), who published his first book on ecumenism, *Chrétiens Dèsunis*, in 1937.[3] Another important ecumenical pioneer was the Dutch priest, Mgr Johannes Willebrands, later Cardinal and the second President of the Vatican Secretariat for Promoting Christian Unity. Mgr Willebrands had been the secretary of the Catholic Conference for Ecumenical Questions from 1952, responsible for gathering Catholic ecumenical pioneers from several countries. From this group came much of the ecumenical re-thinking that influenced Vatican II and the leaders to carry forward the Council's vision for unity.

Couturier provided the spiritual grounding for the later Catholic participation in the ecumenical movement, effecting a revolution in the approach to prayer for Christian unity. Prior to Couturier, the so-called Octave of Prayer for Church Unity was explicitly a prayer for other churches to return to the Roman obedience, and thus could hardly attract the support of more than a tiny handful of non-Catholic Christians. Couturier sought a formula whereby, without compromise, all Christians could pray in the same way for unity – and this at a time when Catholics weren't even allowed to pray the Our Father with non-Catholics. He found this basis in the high-priestly prayer of Jesus in John's Gospel 'that they may all be one; even as, Father, you are in me, and I in you, that they also may be in us, so that the world may believe that you have sent me' (John 17:21). Couturier's formula was that all Christians should pray for the unity that Christ wills by the means that he wills. Probably more than anyone else, Couturier helped to shift the Catholic Church from a church-centred approach to a Christ-centred approach within a thoroughly ecclesial framework.

Couturier had a particular influence on the Decree on Ecumenism of Vatican II. In paragraphs 6-8 of the decree, the Catholic Church clearly endorsed Couturier's teaching on the centrality of prayer, conversion and renewal in the work for unity. 'This change of heart and holiness of life, along with public and private prayer for the unity of Christians, should be regarded as the soul of the whole ecumenical movement and merits the name, "spiritual ecumenism".[4] The name 'spiritual ecumenism' was that chosen by Couturier to describe his apostolate.

The charismatic renewal and Christian unity

We need now to look at the experience of renewal in the Spirit. It is not hard to see that charismatic renewal had a strong ecumenical dimension from the start. This renewal in the Spirit has been happening in virtually all Christian churches across the world.[5] The major characteristics of charismatic renewal have been the same in all the churches: baptism in the Spirit[6] and spiritual gifts; corporate praise, empowering of all believers, evangelism and witness, knowing that God speaks to his people, deliverance and healing ministry, a heightened sense of the prophetic, the raising of eschatological hope.

We see that Christians baptised or filled with the Holy Spirit recognise the work of the Holy Spirit in each other. When they gather, they find that they can readily pray and worship together. Many who became leaders in charismatic renewal were baptised in the Spirit through the ministry of Christians from other Churches.[7] From the beginning of charismatic renewal, there has been a remarkable development in many forms of inter-church sharing that were unknown before: exchanges of teachers, with vast sales of charismatic books by leading teachers, exchange of music ministries, people ministering together, ecumenical prayer groups and communities.

Catholic charismatic renewal understood itself from the start as a fruit of the Second Vatican Council, which had finished only fifteen months before the outbreak at Duquesne and South Bend in the spring of 1967. The movement began predominantly in US student milieux that had been excited by the Vatican II vision for the renewal of the Catholic Church. They immediately understood the new thing they were experiencing as renewal in and through the Spirit for the sake of the Church. They understood the ecumenical dimension, present from the start, as a fruit of the Council's decree on Ecumenism.

This conviction differentiated Catholic charismatic renewal from the movement in many Protestant contexts. Some Protestant charismatics came from evangelical backgrounds that were suspicious of the ecumenical movement. Others, though not so suspicious of ecumenism, did not have so strong a conviction at that time that the charismatic movement was a grace for the renewal of their church.

As a movement of the Holy Spirit, the charismatic movement has pushed God's ecumenical project forward in significant ways. First of all, through charismatic renewal the Holy Spirit has planted a strong impulse for unity among ordinary members of the Church. It directly addressed one of the long-standing weaknesses of the ecumenical movement: that it had remained largely an affair of church leaders and theologians, of the theologically educated and of professionals in the Church, and had never really succeeded in enthusing the Christian masses.[8] Charismatic renewal is above all a grass-roots movement involving millions of believers, most of them without special education, training and qualifications. It is also a trans-church movement touching Christians of almost every known church, denomination or tradition. It has thus had a potential to open up inter-church contacts at the popular level on a vast scale.

Secondly, through charismatic renewal, the Holy Spirit was giving a strong impulse for unity that arose from a renewed relationship with God. Unity was not the goal of charismatic renewal, it was a fruit. Christians seeking the Lord were finding a new level of unity. Here too charismatic renewal contained a corrective to patterns within the ecumenical movement where unity could become an end in itself, a technical task, separated from living faith and the renewal of the Church.

Thirdly, through gifts of praise and spontaneous worship, the Holy Spirit has been enabling Christians from all backgrounds to share together in profound praise and adoration of the Lord. We know each other as sons and daughters in the presence of our common Father. This common worship produces the deep conviction that we belong together; it shows that what we share is far more profound and deep than what divides us; and it provides a deeper motivation for the pursuit of full communion.

Fourthly, the grace of the Spirit in this renewal is bridging one of the biggest gaps in the Christian world, that gap between the Catholic Church and the Evangelical-Pentecostal world. This is where antagonism is deepest today, where there is the strongest tendency towards mutual rejection and condemnation. We Catholics are tempted to denounce the revivalist groupings as 'sects', while they are tempted to dismiss the

Catholic Church as apostate and dead, even to call it a 'cult'. One of the striking works of the Holy Spirit in bridging this chasm is the way in which dedicated Christians on both sides have been led to repentance for their hostility to each other, and given a real respect and a love in their hearts: Evangelical/Pentecostal for Catholic; Catholic for Evangelical/Pentecostal. One of the best known examples is the deep reconciliation and friendship between the Catholic Matteo Calisi and the Pentecostal Giovanni Traettino, that has led to an annual Catholic-Evangelical conference in Italy and to their witnessing together in many countries.

The ecumenical movement and charismatic renewal

One might have expected that this movement of the Spirit with a marked inter-church dimension and remarkable new forms of sharing in worship, ministry and teaching would have given a new dynamism to the ecumenical movement and been welcomed by committed ecumenists. In fact, the ecumenical movement and charismatic renewal have tended to go their own ways. There has been, at least until recently, relatively little interaction between the charismatic movement and the ecumenical movement, and between the official ecumenism of the Catholic Church and the ecumenical dimension of Catholic charismatic renewal.[9]

On the whole, the ecumenists have tended to dismiss charismatic renewal as somewhat of a fringe phenomenon, the preserve of mindless enthusiasts, prone to a fundamentalist reading of scripture. They have probably seen charismatic renewal as at least as divisive as it is unitive, a feature of the charismatic movement to which participants have not paid enough attention.

The charismatics from their side have often not shown much interest in ecumenical activities, and have not involved themselves much in local ecumenical structures such as Churches Together, Councils of Churches, etc. The emphasis of the charismatics has been 'spiritual'; they have frequently seen the ecumenists as insufficiently spiritual and as too absorbed in theological and ecclesiastical affairs.[10]

The failure of the ecumenists to take charismatic renewal seriously as a force for unity is illustrated by the Ecumenical Directory issued in 1993 by the Pontifical Council for Promoting the Unity of Christians. This document has a section on praying together, but it makes no reference to ecumenical sharing in charismatic groups and has no mention of the ways in which charismatic worship and ministry have opened up new levels of ecumenical sharing.

The lack of interaction between the ecumenical movement and charismatic renewal has probably weakened both movements. Certainly by the 1980s, the ecumenical movement had largely lost its spiritual impetus and there was an increasing feeling in ecumenical circles of the movement having run out of steam. While there had been remarkable progress in some theological dialogues, especially with the Lutherans[11] and the Anglicans, as well as in the Faith and Order document, 'Baptism, Eucharist, Ministry' (1982), the dynamism towards unity had slackened, and the process of translating theological progress into church reconciliation seemed slow and difficult. It was as though the ecumenical movement had focused on the head, while the charismatic movement was focused on the heart. In a healthy body, however, the head and the heart function in harmony with each other.

A new forward thrust

In the 1990s, the Holy Spirit has increased the momentum towards Christian unity. Initially, there were further grounds for discouragement: the prospects for Anglican-Catholic reconciliation were set back by the ordination of women in the Anglican communion, and Catholic-Orthodox relations experienced a severe crisis through the resurrection of the Eastern Catholic Churches, often known as the Uniate Churches, following the collapse of Communism. In this humanly unpromising situation, Pope John Paul II has been affirming the Catholic Church's ecumenical commitment with even greater insistence.

The Pope's strong reaffirmation of the commitment of the Catholic Church to ecumenism is most evident in his encyclical letter *Ut unum sint* of 1995. At the beginning, the Pope makes what I believe to be a unique statement in papal documents, namely that he is writing this encyclical 'with the profound conviction that I am obeying the Lord' (para. 4). Although he does not mention the Holy Spirit explicitly in this paragraph, he is in effect saying that in writing this encyclical he is responding to an invitation of the Spirit of God. In line with this beginning, Pope John Paul emphasises the role of the Holy Spirit throughout *Ut unum sint*. He is in fact bringing together once again the theological and spiritual dimensions that had characterised the Catholic ecumenical pioneers and that had found expression in the Council's Decree on Ecumenism. So although he does not mention charismatic renewal, the Holy Father is in fact taking up the issues dear to charismatic Christians that have been missing or only weakly present in the contemporary ecumenical movement.

In the second section of *Ut unum sint*, John Paul II looks at the fruit of the various ecumenical dialogues instituted after Vatican II, saying: 'An overall view of the last thirty years enables us better to appreciate many of the fruits of this common conversion to the gospel which the Spirit of God has brought about by means of the ecumenical movement' (para. 41). The Holy Father then cites various examples of these fruits of the Spirit: transformed attitudes to each other, mutual recognition of baptism, joint translations of the Bible, recognition of each other's witness, especially that of the martyrs.

But the Spirit-awareness of *Ut unum sint* is most clearly shown, not by the number of references to the Holy Spirit, but to the prominence given to the spiritual character of the ecumenical task. There is a stronger emphasis on joint prayer, seemingly influenced by the Pope's experience of praying with other church leaders. He says: 'Fellowship in prayer leads people to look at the Church and Christianity in a new way' (para. 23). The Pope speaks of ecumenical dialogue as an 'examination of conscience', emphasising the close relationship between prayer and dialogue. Here he opens up Catholic practice of ecumenism to expressions of repentance for Catholic sins, which will be the subject of chapter 7.

Towards the end of the encyclical, the Pope returns to the centrality of spiritual ecumenism and the witness to holiness of life. In this context, he introduces a new dimension to ecumenical reflection: he speaks of the importance of Christian martyrs for the unity of the Church. There have, in fact, been more Christian martyrs in the twentieth century than in all the previous nineteen centuries put together, martyrs who have come from every Christian tradition, as the Pope recognises (para. 83). The Catholic Church acknowledges a real communion in Christ with members of other Christian churches and communities, but it remains imperfect until full communion and organic unity is recovered. But the Holy Father says: 'This communion is already perfect in what we all consider the highest point of the life of grace, *martyria* unto death, the truest communion possible with Christ who shed his blood' (para. 84).

The Pope roots his confidence for full reconciliation in the witness of the martyrs and the saints from all Christian traditions. They are the ones who have followed the same Lord Jesus and have experienced the same triumph over evil in and through the blood of Jesus. 'Where there is a sincere desire to follow Christ, the Spirit is often able to pour out his grace in extraordinary ways.' Where Christian communities are able to enter on the way of unity through conversion 'God will do for them what he did for their Saints' (para. 84).

In Rome, the celebration of the Great Jubilee of the Year 2000 has witnessed some remarkable ecumenical developments. On the Feast of the Epiphany, an Orthodox archbishop and Dr George Carey, the Archbishop of Canterbury, took part in the solemn opening of the Holy Door in the Basilica of St Paul. On 7th May, there was an ecumenical celebration in the Colosseum honouring the martyrs of many different traditions in the presence of their representatives. These signs are portents of graces to come.

The Catholic Church is truly becoming more ecumenical through the grace of the Holy Spirit. This desire for unity and this commitment for reconciliation do not arise from the rate of progress, but from the desire of Jesus communicated to the Church through the Holy Spirit. Because of the Holy Spirit, the thrust towards unity is intensifying even if, institutionally, progress seems slow.

Chapter Seven

The Holy Spirit makes the Church more Ecumenical

II: Towards a humble and repentant Church

As the Holy Spirit makes the Church more ecumenical, the Spirit is leading the Church to humility and repentance. Just as sin has produced division and hostility, so the grace of repentance heals division and replaces hostility with respect and love. Only the Holy Spirit can prompt, inspire and effect this process of repentance and reconciliation.

Opening up to repentance

Pope John Paul II has shown immense courage in leading the Catholic Church on the road of repentance. The path to unity requires patience and boldness. The Vatican II Decree on Ecumenism was, as we have seen, a bold and revolutionary initiative, reversing the mentalities of many centuries. But in that first opening of the Catholic Church to an ecumenical vision, it was too soon to raise the question of Catholic repentance for the sins of our past, for the sins that contributed to division and for the resulting sins of calumny and enmity. The Council decree acknowledged that 'often enough' in the church divisions of the past, 'men of both sides were to blame'.[1] It even stated: 'If, in various times and circumstances, there have been deficiencies in moral conduct or in Church discipline, or even in the way the Church teaching has been formulated - to be carefully distinguished from the deposit of faith itself - these should be set right at the opportune moment and in the proper way.'[2] But the decree said nothing about expressions of repentance and asking those offended for forgiveness.

We can easily understand why the Catholic Church has found it hard to open herself up to confessions of sin and weakness. In the post-Reformation polarisation between Catholic and Protestant, the Catholic Church emphasised her God-given authority, understood her teaching as irreformable, inculcated a love of the Church that regarded criticism as disloyalty, and saw reunion as the others confessing their errors and returning to mother Church. From such a background, there are big fears that any Catholic confession of fault will scandalise the faithful and undermine the authority of the Church.

The first big step of humility from the Catholic side was taken by Pope Paul VI during his historic pilgrimage to Jerusalem in 1965. There the Pope and Patriarch Athenagoras of Constantinople made a common confession as they lifted the excommunications of the year 1054: 'They regret the offensive words, the reproaches without foundation and the reprehensible gestures which on both sides marked or accompanied the sad events of that period.'[3]

In general, however, ecumenical dialogues and ecumenical collaboration developed without directly addressing the sins of the past. One important exception has been the *Groupe des Dombes* in France, founded by the Abbé Couturier in 1937. This group of theologians from the Catholic and Protestant Churches have met annually at the Abbey of Notre Dame des Dombes, hence the name of the group. In line with Couturier's inspiration, the theological discussions have been accompanied by prayer together. In 1991, the *Groupe des Dombes* issued a statement entitled *For the Conversion of the Churches*.[4] This document contains one of the most detailed studies to date on the conversion needed in our churches if true reconciliation is to be achieved. It studies the components of our church identities, and asks what needs to change in our identities so as to purify us of elements that are not compatible with the gospel of Jesus.[5] It is worth remarking that the *Groupe des Dombes*, the one ecumenical encounter that has addressed the conversion of the churches, has since produced a most remarkable statement on the ecumenically sensitive issue of Mary, the mother of Jesus.

Preparation for the new millennium

Pope John Paul II has integrated and emphasized the issue of repentance for past sins within the very framework of preparation for the new millennium and the celebration of the Great Jubilee of the Year 2000. In the scriptures, a jubilee celebration is not just an important anniversary. It is a time of restoration. 'And you shall hallow the fiftieth year, and proclaim liberty throughout the land to all its inhabitants; it shall be a jubilee for you, when each of you shall return to his property and each of you shall return to his family' (Lev. 25:10). In the jubilee year, slaves had to be set free and property restored to its original owner. The second millennium since the year 1000 has been a time of serious divisions in the Church. The Holy Father sees the Great Jubilee of the Year 2000 as God's time for healing the wounds of the last millennium and for restoration of the full organic visible unity of the body of Christ. 'It is fitting that the Church should make this passage with a clear awareness of what has happened to her during the last ten centuries. She cannot cross the threshold of the new millennium without encouraging her children to purify themselves through repentance of past errors and instances of infidelity, inconsistency and slowness to act' (*Tertio millennio adveniente*, para. 33). The first category of sins that have weakened the life of the Church to be listed are 'those which have been detrimental to the unity willed by God for his people' (para. 34).

The Holy Father returned to this theme of repentance in his encyclical letter on ecumenism, *Ut unum sint*. Here the Pope introduces a new component into ecumenical dialogue: dialogue as a corporate examination of conscience. Referring to 1 John 1:10, he says: 'Such a radical exhortation to acknowledge our condition as sinners ought also to mark the spirit which we bring to ecumenical dialogue' (para. 34). Here the Pope brings the Church's relationship to God into his vision for ecumenical encounter. 'Dialogue cannot take place merely on a horizontal level, being restricted to meetings, exchanges of points of view or even the sharing of gifts proper to each community. It also has a primarily vertical thrust, directed towards the one who, as the Redeemer of the world and the Lord of history, is himself our reconciliation' (para. 35). From this God-centred vision comes a deep spiritual insight: it is the acknowledgement that 'we are men and women who have sinned... which creates in brothers and sisters living in communities not in full communion with each other that interior space where Christ, the source of the Church's unity, can effectively act, with all the power of his Spirit, the Paraclete' (para. 35).

Let us look a bit more closely at this 'interior space' where Jesus heals and reconciles with the power of the Holy Spirit. When we sin against each other, whether with physical or verbal violence, we cause wounds that act as barriers to trust and communication. We become closed in on ourselves in hurt, suspicion and hostility. The wounds prevent us from seeing the face of Christ in the other who wounded us. The wounds diminish us as Christians. We are less free to act in the Spirit of Christ and we yield easily to a spirit of judgement and condemnation.

Only the Holy Spirit can break into our isolation, whether of oneself, family, tribe or nation, or Church. The Spirit, that flows from the suffering servant who died for our sins, is the one who softens the hard heart, opens the closed mind and gently restores the wounded ego. The Holy Spirit reminds us of our position as sinners purchased through divine love by the blood of the Redeemer. In the infinite love of the Father, who gave his only-begotten Son, we can let go of our defensive arrogance and admit our sin. In this loving way the

Holy Spirit does not humiliate, but humbles; the Spirit does not condemn, but convicts of sin. By the light of God, we are interiorly convicted of our responsibility, and are given the grace to confess. This is the conviction of which Jesus spoke: 'When he [the Counsellor] comes, he will convince the world concerning sin and righteousness and judgement' (John 16:8).

When we are humbled in this way, and are led to confess our sin, the other party with whom we have been in conflict is set free to respond in a godly way. This is the 'interior space' of which the Pope speaks. When we speak aggressively, the other is forced into defensiveness. When we speak with pride, the other party feels justified in their judgement. We confirm the bad things they think about us. When we ignore them, they feel justified in ignoring us. But even when civilised conversation is restored, the underlying wounds are not fully healed until there has been explicit confession and acknowledgement of the sin in our past behaviour. Our confession opens up this 'interior space' in the other to enable them to approach us, opening up the possibility of a new trust, knowing that we have seen what we did in the past and have turned our back on such behaviour.

12th March, 2000

These writings of the Pope were preparing for the Catholic Church's celebration of the Great Jubilee. The Church's repentance for the sins of the past found expression in a remarkable liturgy that took place in Rome, in St Peter's Basilica, on the first Sunday of Lent, 12th March, 2000. The official news release speaks of 'a primatial act' of Pope John Paul II in confessing 'the sins of Christians over the centuries'. 'The Church is a communion of saints, but a solidarity in sin also exists among all the members of the people of God: the bearers of the Petrine ministry, bishops, priests, religious and lay faithful.'[6]

In this penitential liturgy, the repentance was expressed in a general introduction by the Holy Father, followed by specific petitions asking for God's forgiveness for different categories of sins. A cardinal or archbishop, holding responsibility for an area relating to the prayer being made, read each petition and each was followed by a request for pardon made by the Pope.

The revolutionary character of this Catholic confession and request for forgiveness has not been adequately brought out in most press reports. The official Vatican commentary itself said: 'Indeed, in the entire history of the Church, there are no precedents for requests for forgiveness by the magisterium for past wrongs.'[7] The pre-Vatican II emphasis was always on 'Catholic truth' in the context of the adage 'error has no rights'. It was assumed that anyone criticising or opposing Church leadership was not in the truth. So it was an amazing sight to see Cardinal Joseph Ratzinger, prefect of the Congregation for the Doctrine of the Faith, the successor of the Roman Inquisition, confessing that 'the sons and daughters of the Church yielded to sentiments of intolerance and committed acts of violence against their brothers and sisters who professed other religious beliefs', asking the Lord to 'forgive us and teach us to proclaim the truth with gentleness and charity'.

The charismatic contribution

In the Catholic Church, it is the Pope who has been setting the pace in making the Church more humble and repentant. In general, the renewal movements in the Catholic Church, including Catholic charismatic renewal, have emphasised the importance of personal repentance for sin as a vital element in all renewal, but they have not said much about repentance for the sins of past centuries as a constitutive element in the renewal of the Church.

However, some of the most striking prophecies in the history of charismatic renewal, given by Catholic leaders at Kansas City in 1977, concerned repentance. Two words directly addressed the sin of Christian division. 'Mourn and weep, for the body of my Son is broken... Come before me with broken hearts and contrite spirits, for the body of my Son is broken. Turn from the sins of your fathers. Walk in the ways of my Son. Return to the plan of your Father, return to the purpose of your God.' Another word was specifically addressed to church leaders: 'You are all guilty in my eyes for the condition of my people, who are weak and divided and unprepared... You have tolerated divisions among yourselves and grown used to it. You have not repented for it or fasted for it or sought me to bring it to an end. You have tolerated it, and you have increased it. And you have not been my servants first of all in every case, but you have served other people ahead of me, and you have served this world ahead of me and you have served your organization ahead of me. But I am God, and you are my servants; why are you not serving me first of all?'[8]

The Pope's initiative for Catholic repentance has a great potential to unblock the obstacles to Christian unity and set loose a new dynamism for renewal and reconciliation. But it faces a similar problem to the ecumenical movement: how to move it from the head to the heart, and from church leaders and theologians to the church public? The Pope has urged that the Vatican liturgy of 12th March be taken as a model to be used and adapted in dioceses throughout the world. But how can we make sure that these noble words become real expressions of the heart and do not remain simply beautiful sentiments on paper? It is here that the charismatic movement can play a very important role as a popular movement and as a movement of the Spirit.

In fact, it is from charismatic circles that very important initiatives for the healing of ancient divisions have developed in the last fifteen years. These initiatives have arisen primarily outside the Catholic Church and mostly in evangelical non-denominational circles. Among the key leaders is John Dawson, a New Zealander who has become a citizen of the USA, and who lived for some twenty years in a largely African-American area of Los Angeles. John Dawson is the founder of the International Reconciliation Coalition, which seeks to co-ordinate and promote reconciliation in all situations of human conflict, particularly through what Dawson calls 'identificational repentance'.[9] Dawson has developed a thorough methodology for addressing ancient conflicts through study of the key events and developments in the origins of each conflict, and a confession of the sin by those identifying with the original perpetrators. This prayerful and repentant approach to ancient conflicts has led to a multiplication of prayer journeys to sites associated with their historical roots.

Among the important prayer journeys has been the YWAM-sponsored Reconciliation Walk for the 900th anniversary of the First Crusade (1095-1099). The walk followed the routes taken by the Crusaders, asking forgiveness from the Muslim, Jewish and Orthodox communities for the atrocities committed. Other highly significant prayer journeys have included one to the old slave ports of West Africa, and another to aborigine sites in Australia. While many of these have focused on racial, tribal and national enmities, the methods being developed are also relevant to the conflicts between divided Christian communities.[10]

Some reasons why these initiatives have been pioneered by charismatic Christians are not hard to see. First, in charismatic prayer, the participants can respond spontaneously and freely to the Holy Spirit, and are not tied to prescribed forms and set words. This freedom of expression is essential for being led more deeply into sensitive areas and situations for which there are no ready-made formulae. Secondly, this freedom of expression includes a freedom of emotional expression. Participants can respond to situations of deep-rooted evil and profound suffering with their hearts and their guts, as well as with their minds. This interior opening of the heart to tears and groaning enables the participants in repentance initiatives to enter into a real grieving over the sins of Christian history. In this grieving, the Holy Spirit enables Christians to enter more deeply into the heart of God the Father. Thirdly, through their experience of the Holy Spirit, charismatic Christians have discovered the reality of evil spirits. As a result, they see that their repentance is not just dealing with long-standing human attitudes, but also with spiritual forces that have become entrenched in the conflict situations and in which they foment ongoing malevolence. As will be evident, these initiatives require mature leadership and are best suited to small groups of experienced intercessors.

The biblical prayer of lamentation

At least in our Western societies, our worship had become so cerebral that we had little idea of the biblical (and deeply Jewish) prayer of lamentation. Perhaps occasionally we see images on television of Jews weeping at the Wailing Wall in Jerusalem, or we see pictures of bereaved mothers weeping over their dead children - but we may not think of their grief as prayer. In the Old Testament, however, laments were a recognised form of prayer that occupied an important place in the worship of Israel.

We find the prayer of lament especially in the book of Lamentations. This book, attributed to the prophet Jeremiah, presents the response of a faithful Jew to the calamity of the destruction of the first temple, the devastation of Jerusalem and the taking of many Jews into exile in Babylon. Some psalms of lament, psalms 74 and 79, also seem to come from the same period.[11] In the book of Lamentations we find the essential ingredients for the repentance of a people for its past sins: identification; acknowledgement; confession; grief/lamentation of heart.

Confession. In lamenting the tragedy of Jerusalem's ruins, the prophet confesses: 'Jerusalem sinned grievously, therefore she became filthy' (Lam. 1:8); 'Your prophets have seen for you false and deceptive visions; they have not exposed your iniquity to restore your fortunes, but have seen for you oracles false and misleading' (Lam. 2:14); 'This was for the sins of her prophets and the iniquities of her priests, who shed in the midst of her the blood of the righteous' (Lam. 4:13).

Identification. The one lamenting is expressing the lament of the people. Indeed many verses are presented as the utterance of Jerusalem: 'My transgressions were bound into a yoke... the Lord gave me into the hands of those whom I cannot withstand' (Lam. 1:14); 'In the dust of the streets lie the young and the old; my maidens and my young men have fallen by the sword' (Lam. 2:21). The prophet identifies with the sinful people: 'The crown has fallen from our head; woe to us, for we have sinned!' (Lam. 5:16).

Grief/lament of the heart. 'For these things I weep; my eyes flow with tears' (Lam. 1:16); 'My eyes are spent with weeping; my soul is in tumult; my heart is poured out in grief because of the destruction of the daughter of my people' (Lam. 2:11). There seems to be a particular form of grieving prayer proper to women, which no doubt reflects both the particular suffering of women as victims of violence, or as mothers or widows, and the deep sensitivity and receptivity that characterize the woman. 'Hear, O women, the word of the Lord, and let your ear receive the word of his mouth; teach to your daughters a lament, and each to her neighbour a dirge' (Jer. 9:20).

The Pope is seeing, along with more Christians, that as long as there has not been an honest confession, a genuine identification and a real grieving over the sins of the past, these evils still have a power to be reactivated today. Many of these deep wounds from over the centuries are expressions of Christian division: between Catholics and Protestants in Northern Ireland, and between Catholics and Orthodox in the former Yugoslavia. Severe conflicts of shorter duration have developed between Catholics and Evangelicals in places such as Chiapas, Southern Mexico and in Colombia. While many other ferocious conflicts are rooted in religion and in ethnic rivalry, the conflicts between Christians have a unique gravity because the hatred in Christian division is a direct counter-witness to the basic Christian gospel, which is a message of reconciliation and forgiveness through the blood and the cross of Jesus Christ. That is why the Holy Spirit is drawing the attention of Christians to these scandals, and prompting initiatives of repentance and forgiveness.

For the sake of Christian unity, therefore, it is of paramount importance that the Catholic Church be humble and repentant. More than any other, this factor will determine whether or not the Church can now enter into a period of profound renewal and enjoy a new springtime of the Spirit.

Chapter Eight

The Holy Spirit makes the Church more Ecumenical

III: The Church and Israel

There is, however, a further ecumenical factor high-lighted by the Holy Spirit - it is the place of Israel, of the Jewish people, in God's plan of salvation. This issue is playing a major part in the Catholic Church adopting a more humble and repentant posture concerning our history.

Some may wonder why I am raising this question under ecumenism and Christian unity. Does the issue of the Jewish people not belong under the heading of non-Christian religions? Despite the fact that, for largely political and procedural reasons, relations with the Jews were treated under non-Christian religions by the Second Vatican Council,[1] it is the Pontifical Council for Promoting the Unity of Christians that handles relations with the Jewish people in the Vatican, not the Council for Non-Christian Religions. The reason for this is that the unity of the Church of God was rooted in Israel. The relationship with the Jews belongs within the covenant God made with his chosen people, unlike relations with believers in other faiths like Buddhism, Hinduism and

Islam. Thus the Catechism teaches: 'When she delves into her own mystery, the Church, the People of God in the New Covenant, discovers her link with the Jewish People, "the first to hear the Word of God". The Jewish faith, unlike other non-Christian religions, is already a response to God's revelation in the Old Covenant' (CCC, para. 839).

The challenge of the Holy Spirit

It is with the Jewish people that we encounter one of the strongest challenges of the Holy Spirit to the Church. In fact, it seems to be this challenge that has spurred the Catholic Church to a repentance for the evils of the past, to an acknowledgement of Catholic responsibility for past patterns of persecution and intolerance. For it is our treatment of the Jews that constitutes the most long-standing reproach to the Church and that represents the most shocking dimension of the Church's history.

The catalyst for Catholic self-examination has been the horrendous evil of the Holocaust, when Nazi Germany exterminated six million Jews in the most organised and 'scientific' attempt ever made to eliminate an entire people. As Christians have awakened slowly to the massive scope of this horror, they have been led to ask how such an evil could have been possible in 'Christian Europe'. This, in turn, has drawn Catholic attention to the long history of anti-semitism in the Catholic Church: to anti-Jewish prejudice, anti-Jewish legislation, exclusion from public life, social marginalisa-tion, baptisms under duress, enforced exile and many forms of violence, mostly by unruly mobs, sometimes incited by inflammatory preaching.

This catalogue of sins committed against the Jewish people provides the groundwork for a first level of Catholic repentance for anti-semitism. At this level, the sin is the sin of racial prejudice, and can be recognised and combatted by any human being of good will. These sins were first addressed by the Second Vatican Council in its Decree on Non-Christian Religions (*Nostra aetate*), where the Church stated that she 'deplores all hatreds, persecutions and displays of anti-semitism levelled at any time or from any source against the Jews' (para. 4).

However, it does not take much historical research to discover that the sins of Catholics against the Jewish people were not simply another form of racism similar to any other. The prejudice, contempt and violence against the Jews had theological roots. They were blamed for the death of Jesus and so they were called 'God-killers'. The misfortunes of the Jewish people were seen as a punishment for their refusal to accept Jesus as their Messiah, and as a sign that God had rejected them, that they were no longer God's chosen people, and the covenant with Israel was no more. The bishops at Vatican II also addressed this theological element in anti-Jewish prejudice: 'The apostle Paul maintains that the Jews remain very dear to God, for the sake of the patriarchs, since God does not take back the gifts he bestowed or the choice he made... It is true that the Church is the new people of God, yet the Jews should not be spoken of as rejected or accursed as if this followed from Holy Scripture' (para. 4).

Here we arrive at a second level of repentance for Catholic sins against the Jewish people: a repentance for the false teaching that God had rejected the Jewish people and revoked his covenant with them because they had rejected Jesus as the Messiah. Although this 'replacement' or 'substitution' teaching was never made the official teaching of the Church, it was the common preaching throughout the centuries, including that of many canonised saints. Here we touch on a basic reason for the virulence and the depth of the anti-Jewish spirit in the Church. The Jews were despised because, it was thought, God had rejected them and condemned them to perpetual humiliation before the nations; and this easily spilled over into the attitude that Gentile believers would do well to ensure that the Jews were kept in this humiliated condition.

Since Vatican II, the Catholic rejection of this false teaching has become even more explicit. Pope John Paul II has spoken several times in very direct terms that God's covenant with Israel has never been revoked. In the first-ever visit of a Pope to a synagogue, John Paul said to the gathered Jews: 'You are our dearly beloved brothers and, in a certain way, it could be said that you are our elder brothers.'[2] In the liturgy of repentance at St Peter's on 12th March, 2000, God was asked to forgive the sins of Catholics against 'the people of the covenant'.

Nevertheless, there would seem to have been more theological change in the Catholic Church at these two levels than heart-repentance. No doubt the Holy Father senses this as, in this year of the Great Jubilee, he calls us Catholics to a real sorrow for our sins against the Jews. The Holy Father's visit to Israel had an extraordinary impact because the Jews of Israel sensed his deep feeling for the sufferings of the Jewish people through the ages and, particularly, in the Holocaust, and the image of the frail and suffering Pope at the Western Wall in Jerusalem, placing the prayer of Catholic repentance between the stones of the wall, will remain a powerful stimulus.

Here again, Christians blessed by God with a freedom of expression in prayer and ministry and endowed with charismatic gifts have a particular responsibility to express the repentance of the whole Church for the Christian oppression of the Jews. I have been privileged to be part of several prayer initiatives in which Protestants and Catholics have humbled themselves before God in acknowledging Christian sins against the Jewish people over the centuries, and together have sought God's way ahead for the future. These events, often lasting several days, have been among the most profound experiences of my Christian life. It is here that I am particularly conscious of the great difference made by the Lord's gift of a new freedom of the Spirit in the Pentecostal and charismatic movements - it is this interior freedom that has enabled us to pray, weep and rejoice together, and to receive the deep groanings of the Holy Spirit who 'helps us in our weakness' (Rom. 8:26).

The Holy Spirit opens up a new stage

It is in relation to the role of the Jewish people in God's plan that the Holy Spirit has been springing some of the biggest surprises. One of these is the rise of the Messianic Jews, that is to say, Jews who confess Jesus of Nazareth as the Messiah of Israel, while continuing to affirm their Jewish identity and live a Jewish lifestyle. What these new Jewish believers in Jesus are saying to us Christians, Orthodox, Catholic and Protestant, is this: when we Jews come to faith in Jesus as our Messiah, the Messiah of Israel, why should we have to reject our Jewishness and become like Gentiles? Why can we not do what the first generation of believers in Jesus did at the origins of the Church? That is, to live as believers who confess Jesus as Messiah, while continuing to live as Jews and be part of Israel.

I believe this emergence of the Messianic Jews to be a work of the Holy Spirit, firstly because such a phenomenon could never have got off the ground from purely human origins. The obstacles are too great. The opposition and fears of the wider Jewish community are deep: they see any movement of Jewish believers in Jesus as yet another Christian missionary device to destroy Judaism and convert Jews to 'Christianity'. The Church tends to be unwelcoming, because Messianic Judaism can seem like yet another revivalist sect, spawning yet more divisions in the body of Christ. To some Christians, it has all the appearance of another Judaising tendency within the Christian fold similar to that condemned by Paul in the letter to the Galatians. In fact, a leading Messianic Jew has said that if there is one thing that synagogue and Church have agreed upon throughout the centuries, it is that Messianic Jews have no right to exist.

The Messianic movement is also a work of the Holy Spirit because its rise has been closely associated with the spread of the wider charismatic movement. Its origins were not totally in the charismatic movement, because over the last century and a quarter there have been a few Jewish believers in Jesus - in Israel, in Moldovia, in the USA - calling for the realisation of this vision: the restoration of the Jewish Church. But until the late 1960s, these visionaries had little success translating dream into reality. It was particularly through the impact of the Holy Spirit in the Jesus 'hippie' movement that many young Jews came to faith in Jesus as their Messiah and Lord. In this charismatic context, with the exercise of the spiritual gifts, a whole new current of dynamic evangelism was launched among Jewish believers in Jesus. As a result, there have been an increasing number of Messianic Jewish congregations established in the USA since the early 1970s and somewhat more recently elsewhere. In Israel, not surprisingly, the Messianic movement has faced the toughest opposition, and its main growth has been in the 1990s, following mass immigration from the former Soviet Union.[3]

Thirdly, the role of the Holy Spirit in the rise of this movement can also be seen in its creativity. The rise of Messianic Judaism is not simply the appearance of a group that worships on Saturdays, with a few distinctive emphases. The vision of being both Jewish and believers in Jesus as Messiah of Israel involves the creation of a distinctive way of life and distinctive forms of worship. What is evolving in Messianic Judaism could not just be the work of church committees of pastors and liturgists without the creative spark of the Spirit of life in the congregations. Their creativity can be seen particularly in their music and in the role of dancing in their worship.

The rise of these Messianic assemblies or synagogues leads, in fact, to one of the greatest challenges to the Church. It faces us with the question: what happened to the Jewish Church of the origins? In Acts 15, the apostles and elders who met together in council were all Jewish believers in Jesus. Within three hundred years, baptised Jews were being required to renounce their Jewishness and to cease all observance of the Jewish calendar, the sabbath and the Jewish feasts. And so this question leads us to a third level of repentance: repentance for the suppression and loss of the Jewish expression of the Church. This third level more directly challenges us as Church, because the decisions requiring Jewish converts to renounce their Jewishness and to cease all Jewish practices were decisions of Church authority, mostly of local synods and councils in various parts of the Roman Empire.[4] The wrongness of this policy, and the immense interior suffering it inflicted on Jewish converts, cannot be dismissed as simply the failings of individual Catholics.

When we examine the question of a Jewish expression of the Church, mention should also be made of the groups of Catholics who are Jewish. A number of Jewish Catholics are now reclaiming their Jewish identity within the communion of the Catholic Church. They generally call themselves Hebrew Catholics, seeking to express their Catholic faith as Jews, particularly with the development of a Hebrew liturgy, not just the use of a

Hebrew translation of the Latin rite. World-wide there is a Hebrew Catholic Association, founded by a Jewish Carmelite priest, Fr Elias Friedman (1916-99), and which is seeking official Church recognition.[5] A small association of Hebrew Catholics in Paris called *Marie, Fille de Sion*, has received the approval of Cardinal Lustiger, the Archbishop of Paris. These Hebrew Catholics have seen in the canonisation of Edith Stein - St Teresa Benedicta of the Cross - a sign of great encouragement, because Edith Stein always affirmed her Jewishness and indeed did so in a striking way when the Gestapo came to arrest her and despatch her to the gas chambers of Auschwitz.

The Jewish church and unity

If you are still wondering why I am treating the Israel question under the heading of ecumenism, we can turn for further light to Paul's teaching in the Letter to the Ephesians. There, in chapter 2, the apostle teaches that the Church is made up of Jew and Gentile: 'For he [Christ] is our peace, who has made us both one and has broken down the wall of hostility' (2:14). The implications of this passage are that the unity of the Church is founded in the reconciliation of Jew and Gentile through the blood of Jesus. The result of Jesus' death on the cross is that 'you [the Gentile believers] are no longer strangers and sojourners, but you are fellow citizens with the saints [the Jewish believers] and members of the household of God' (2:19). Paul repeats this same teaching at the beginning of chapter 3, where he speaks of the 'mystery of Christ, which was not made known to the sons of men in other generations as it has now been revealed to his holy [Jewish] apostles and prophets by the Spirit; that is, how the Gentiles are fellow heirs, members of the same body, and partakers of the promise in Christ Jesus through the gospel' (3:4-6).

If the union of Jew and Gentile in the one body was foundational for the Church's unity, then the loss of the Jewish Church was a catastrophe for unity, and its suppression was the infliction of a deep wound on the body of Christ. The tragedy of this loss can be further grasped when we look at Romans 11, where Paul speaks of the Gentile believers as wild olive branches grafted into the natural olive tree. The natural olive is clearly faithful Israel, Israel faithful to the God of Abraham, Isaac and Jacob, and faithful to the Messiah of Israel. In the light of Romans, the union spoken of in Ephesians is not simply the conjoining of two disparate groups, but the bringing in of one group, the Gentiles, into the covenantal reality already established and renewed with the other, Israel.

The Messianic Jews and Christian unity

At first sight, it might seem that the Messianic Jews add to the problems of Christian division, because they represent yet another grouping of believers in Jesus, and one that is hardly united in itself. However, my experience of recent years has shown me that whenever Catholics and Protestants are gathered together in prayer with Messianic Jews, a deeper reconciliation occurs between the Catholics and the Protestants. It is worth reflecting on the dynamic of such encounters and how they advance this deeper reconciliation.

When they meet with Messianic Jews, Gentile Christians are faced with a people who have suffered:

as Jews they have suffered the persecutions and pogroms with their fellow Jews; while at the same time, as believers in Jesus, they have had their Jewishness denied by their fellow Jews. In this situation, Catholics and Protestants find themselves humbled before their Jewish brethren. This totally removes the usual, even if hidden, rivalry and self-justification, each thinking they are right as against the other. In confessing our own sin against the Jews in general and against Jewish believers in Jesus, each is truly humbled and recognises the first place of the Jew in the body of Messiah. We may not yet understand what this first place means in practice, but together we can recognise God's order expressed by St Paul: 'to the Jew first and also to the Greek' (Rom. 1:16).

When divided Christians discover that they are being brought closer through the presence of the Jew, particularly by the Jewish believer in Jesus, then we can perhaps get a new glimpse of the priestly calling of the Jewish people in relation to all the nations of the earth. It belongs to the very calling of Israel to be God's instrument to bless all the peoples of the world. God's choice of one is for the sake of all. In fact, the common humbling of Gentile Christians before the Jewish believers in Jesus opens up once again this distinctively Jewish ministry to the Church of the nations.

What does this mean for the unity of the Church?

It is difficult at this stage to say much about the implications of Catholic repentance for our sins against the Jews, and the unexpected reappearance of Jewish expressions of the body of Christ/Messiah. It is too early to say more than that we are living in momentous days: days in which things unimaginable to our forefathers are happening. Much that was unimaginable has involved the remarkable figure of Pope John Paul II and his initiatives concerning the Jewish people: the numerous messages he has addressed to leaders of Jewish communities around the world, his visit to the synagogue of Rome, his pilgrimage to the land of Israel.

It must be true that the historic opening of the Catholic Church to a humble acknowledgement of the evils of the past will have spiritual effects beyond what we can now imagine. The repentance for sins against the Jews is at the heart of this humbling, and the resulting fruit will do more than anything else for the unity of the whole body. The Holy Father must have some inkling of the connection between his initiatives concerning the Jewish people and the 'new springtime'[6] for the Church of which he has spoken in connection with the Great Jubilee and the start of a new millennium.

We can say that the Holy Spirit is taking us right back to the beginning, to the foundations. This is not so that we will copy first or second century patterns in a form of archaeological reconstruction, but so that the Holy Spirit can bring us back to the core, to the heart of the biblical revelation and its supreme manifestation in the incarnate Son of God, who is son of Abraham, son of David and son of Mary. This is surely another dimension of the Holy Spirit as 'the living memory of the Church': that the Holy Spirit will ultimately not allow the Church to forget her origins in Israel, the day of Pentecost, the full range of spiritual gifts and her authentic catholicity that is grounded in the universal call of Israel and of Jerusalem.

I can, perhaps, add that the return to the Jewish roots can surely be the only way to address the ecumenically difficult question of Mary, the mother of Jesus. The return to the roots involves learning to re-read the scriptures in the light of the calling of Israel. Mary cannot be properly understood except as a Jewish girl, as Daughter of Zion, as the virgin who embodies in a unique way the calling of Israel to give birth to the Messiah and Saviour. Re-connecting with the Jewish roots will replace Mary in the soil of Israel, and make possible first a convergence and then a reconciliation between those Christians for whom she is the deeply honoured Mother of God and those for whom Marian devotion represents a pagan defilement of the gospel.

Thus the Holy Spirit makes the Church more ecumenical, first, in stirring up the desire for unity and awareness of the sin of division; secondly, by leading the Church to a humble repentance for the sins against unity; and thirdly by leading the Church back to her roots in the Jewish Messiah and to her unity as the 'one new man', formed of Jew and Gentile, with all mutual hostility destroyed by the cross.

Chapter Nine

The Holy Spirit makes the Church more Eschatological

I: Restoring the hope of the Church

Before my involvement in charismatic renewal, the second coming of Jesus was something I believed in, but never thought about. Consequently I never preached about it, even in Advent. It was an 'external' truth that did not touch my inner life. I thought of people who got excited about the last days as fanatical and weird. At best, eschatology was a theological topic that could be interesting, as long as it avoided all fundamentalism and *naïveté*.

This indifference to the second coming of Jesus began to melt when I experienced a deep renewal in my faith through charismatic renewal. Although it took a few years for 'the penny to drop', I can see in retrospect that the seeds of a new hope had been sown. A renewed faith in the living Lordship of Jesus Christ leads naturally to a renewed faith in his second coming and the fulness of his reign in the coming kingdom. So as I began to turn my gaze more towards future life in God, I found the Holy Spirit bringing alive the 'blessed hope, the appearing of the glory of our great God and Saviour Jesus Christ' (Tit. 2:13).

In fact, the gift of the Holy Spirit will always sow the blessed hope. The gift of the Spirit is the gift of the risen Lord. He is pouring out that which he has received totally into his humanity. 'Being therefore exalted at the right hand of God, and having received from the Father the promise of the Holy Spirit, he has poured out this which you see and hear' (Acts 2:33). The glorification of Jesus in his resurrection-ascension represents the total penetration of his humanity by the Holy Spirit. The Spirit penetrates and fills every part and dimension of the body of Jesus. When we receive the Holy Spirit into ourselves, we receive the seed and the promise of our own glorification. What Jesus now is as glorified man, so also shall we be.

The gift of the Holy Spirit as first fruits

Perhaps the key that opened up the whole area of the second coming was the discovery of St Paul's teaching on the gift of the Holy Spirit as *aparchē* (first fruits) and as *arrabōn* (deposit). In the charismatic movement, with its accent on an experiential reception of the Spirit, the emphasis was all on receiving the Holy Spirit. It was easy to assume that receiving the Holy Spirit meant receiving everything now. It was therefore a wonderful corrective to receive light from these passages about first-fruits and deposit. These passages both convey the greatness of the present gift of the Holy Spirit, and the vastness of what is to come, which is heralded by the present gift.

Maybe it is best to start from 2 Corinthians, because this epistle particularly addresses the paradox of the Christian life: the paradox that 'we have this treasure [the Holy Spirit] in earthen vessels' (2 Cor. 4:7), the paradox that 'death is at work in us, but life in you' (2 Cor. 4:12), the paradox that the man 'caught up to the third heaven' (2 Cor. 12:2) is the man who has suffered 'far greater labours, far more imprisonments, with countless beatings, and often near death' (2 Cor. 11:23), the paradox that 'when I am weak, then I am strong' (2 Cor. 12:10).

Twice in 2 Corinthians, in very similar passages, St Paul speaks of *ton arrabōn tou pneumatos*, the earnest or the deposit of the Spirit. First, he writes: 'He has put his seal upon us and given us his Spirit in our hearts as a guarantee' (1:22) and then later that God 'has given us the Spirit as a guarantee' (5:5). We will look in a moment at the important image of being sealed.[1] The clear sense of this language of deposit or guarantee is that the Christian is given a first taste of the Spirit, of which the fulness is yet to come.

It is in 2 Corinthians 5 that St Paul develops this relationship between the present gift and the fulness to come. Here in this age we live in an 'earthly tent' that is liable to destruction (5:1), evidently the human body. So, he says, 'here indeed we groan, and long to put on our heavenly dwelling' (5:2). Here we find a paradoxical result of receiving the Spirit: we begin to groan. Yes, the gift of the Spirit does bring joy, but it also brings groaning. The first taste of the Spirit of God gives us a desire and a longing for the fulness. The gift of the Spirit makes us aware of the contrast, at times painful, between the gift God gives and the receptacle into which the gift is poured, the contrast between the treasure and the earthen vessel. In this situation, we 'long to put on our heavenly clothing', that is to say, we long for the spiritual body of the resurrection.

St Paul continues: 'For while we are still in this tent, we sigh with anxiety; not that we would be unclothed, but that we would be further clothed, so that what is mortal may be swallowed up by life' (5:4). The situation of the Christian in this world, of having the treasure of the Holy Spirit in a mortal body, is one of tension: a tension between the Spirit that brings an indestructible life and the body that is heading towards the grave. In chapter 4, which is packed with examples of this paradox, Paul says that 'Though our outer nature is wasting away, our inner nature is being renewed every day' (2 Cor. 4:16). This situation of tension gives rise to a longing for deliverance: most basically, a longing for deliverance from mortality but also a deliverance from sin, temptation and weakness. But in this tension we do not just experience a human desire to be rid of it. It is the Holy Spirit bringing us the taste of God that is the assurance of future deliverance and that issues in a deep longing. But the longing for the kingdom includes a longing for an end to temptation, moral ambiguity, conflict, constant tension, sickness and the decline of old age. We do not want to be 'found naked' (5:3) or 'unclothed' (5:4), that is to say, to die before the resurrection, and suffer the loss of our bodies. We want our mortal existence to be overtaken, to be swallowed up, by the glory of the resurrection of the body. 'When the perishable puts on the imperishable, and the mortal puts on immortality, then shall come to pass the saying that is written: "Death is swallowed up in victory"' (1 Cor. 15:54).

St Paul finishes the verses in 2 Corinthians 5 with the statement that God 'has prepared us for this very thing' (5:5), that is, for the glory of the resurrection, of which the initial gift of the Spirit is a first taste and a guarantee. This is not to be understood as a personal guarantee of a new salvation for every believer whatever his future behaviour, a view which St Paul elsewhere rejects,[2] but as a statement that (i) the gift of the Spirit is an infallible sign of God's determination to save the whole person in the resurrection and, (ii), the gift of the Spirit is already preparing the individual believer and the church community for the resurrection to come. This will certainly follow unless the believer decisively rejects this gift.

In Romans 8, St Paul uses the language of 'first fruits' to describe the initial gift of the Spirit: 'Not only the creation, but we ourselves, who have the first fruits of the Spirit, groan inwardly as we wait for adoption as sons, the redemption of our bodies' (8:23). This is really the same teaching as in 2 Corinthians 5, with some variations of terminology. Again, we find the language of groaning, and again the groaning is related to our bodies and their final salvation.

Romans 8 adds a dimension to St Paul's teaching on the groaning of the Christian. In verse 26, he writes: 'Likewise the Spirit helps us in our weakness; for we do not know how to pray as we ought, but the Spirit intercedes for us with sighs too deep for words.' In fact, the Greek word translated here as 'sighs' has the same root as the word used in verse 23, 'we groan inwardly as we wait for adoption as sons'. So it is very unlikely that the groaning of the Christian is unrelated to the sighing or groaning of the Holy Spirit. This suggests that the 'weakness' of verse 26 is our situation as Christians on earth awaiting the resurrection, of having the 'treasure in earthen vessels'. That is to say, we do not know how to pray for the second coming, but the Holy Spirit's groaning comes to our aid to enable us to groan and long with the depth and the power of the Spirit of God.

Here, in Romans 8, St Paul speaks of this 'redemption of our bodies' as 'our adoption as sons' (8:23). Does this mean we only become sons of God in the resurrection? It would seem not, since St Paul has said a few verses earlier: 'For all who are led by the Spirit of God are sons of God' (8:14) and 'you have received the spirit of sonship' (8:15). But surely he is seeing our clothing with the spiritual body of the resurrection as the completion of our sonship, an idea that seems to be implied when he speaks of 'the creation' obtaining 'the glorious liberty of the children of God' (8:21).

Being sealed

The idea of 'first fruits' and 'deposit' are closely linked with 'being sealed'. Besides 2 Corinthians 1:22, this link is found in Ephesians 1:13-14, where we read: 'you... were sealed with the promised Holy Spirit, which is the guarantee of our inheritance.'[3] A seal bears the image of the one whose authority it represents, so that what is marked with the seal becomes the possession or property of the one whose image it bears.[4] The imagery of being stamped with a seal refers to an identifiable event in the life of the Christian: in Ephesians 1, the reference is to Christian initiation, to baptism-confirmation. But this marking with the seal makes a deep imprint on the deepest point of our being. The seal is both visible in its imposition and invisible in its deepest effects.

The image of God is Christ (Col. 1:15). The Holy Spirit is the instrument of the sealing (Eph. 1:13). So the seal means that through the Holy Spirit we are stamped with the life of Christ, and we become the property and the sons of the Father. This fits with St Paul's language in 2 Corinthians about our 'being changed into his likeness from one degree of glory to another' (3:18).

But the sealing is in view of the coming kingdom. The Holy Spirit by which we are sealed is 'the Holy Spirit of promise', that is 'the guarantee of our inheritance', literally 'unto [the] redemption of possession, to the praise of his glory' (Eph. 1:14).[5] We are sealed as a sign marking us out for the day when we will become in full reality the redeemed possession of our God. This point is made clear later in Ephesians: 'Do not grieve the Holy Spirit of God, by whom you were sealed for the day of redemption' (4:30). Here the relationship between the sealing and the day of the resurrection is made explicit. We are sealed in view of the day of redemption. Our life is now ordered to that day. That is why we grieve the Spirit of God, when we act in any way that denies that destiny, that blocks or delays the coming of the day of redemption.

Salvation in the New Testament

The blessed hope of the Lord's coming and of his kingdom is the blessed hope of our salvation. In the New

Testament, the noun *sōtēria*, salvation, normally refers to the full deliverance of the resurrection from the dead. This holistic understanding of salvation is typically Jewish. For the people of Israel, human existence is essentially a bodily existence. There is something very earthy about Jewish faith. The human person was created as an embodied spirit, united in body and soul. Our bodies are central to our existence and our identity. It was sin that led to death, the sundering of the human person, the separation of soul from body. That is why St Paul calls death an enemy. God's salvation rescues us from all the consequences of sin. Thus, in the Jewish biblical view, human salvation could not be full salvation without the salvation of the body. This happens in the resurrection, when St Paul's prophecy is fulfilled: 'The last enemy to be destroyed is death' (1 Cor. 15:26).

So, when Paul speaks of the Lord's coming in 1 Thessalonians, he writes: 'For God has not destined us for wrath, but to obtain salvation through our Lord Jesus Christ' (1 Thess. 5:9). In 2 Timothy, he writes: 'Therefore I endure everything for the sake of the elect, that they also may obtain salvation in Christ Jesus with its eternal glory' (2 Tim. 2:10). So, when he says in the next chapter that the scriptures are 'able to instruct you for salvation through faith in Christ Jesus' (2 Tim. 3:15), he is saying that the scriptures have the power and the capacity to prepare Christians for the coming of the Lord and his kingdom.

The author of Hebrews speaks of the difference between the two comings of Jesus. In his first coming, 'he has appeared once and for all at the end of the age to put away sin by the sacrifice of himself' (Heb. 9:26). But Christ 'will appear a second time, not to deal with sin, but to save those who are eagerly waiting for him' (Heb. 9:28).[6] We find the same usage in 1 Peter: 'By his great mercy we have been born anew to a living hope... to an inheritance... kept in heaven for you, who by God's power are guarded through faith for a salvation ready to be revealed in the last time' (1 Peter 1:3-5).

Renewal and the *Parousia*

The basic link between the experience of spiritual renewal and the awakening of hope for the second coming of Jesus lies in the gift of the Holy Spirit. As we welcome the gift of the Spirit in this life, we experience a desire for the fulness of the gift of the Spirit in the resurrection. This longing and desire can only be awoken by the Holy Spirit. 'Come' is the cry of the Spirit and of the bride (Rev. 22:17); it is the cry that the Spirit teaches to the bride.

The Spirit awakens this hope in the individual Christian and in the Church. As this hope is awakened, the Christian discovers that this longing for the Parousia (the second coming) and the kingdom is mentioned as frequently as any other doctrine in the New Testament. We become aware of how this hope suffuses the Catholic liturgy. It is found in acclamations after the consecration,[7] in Eucharistic Prayer no.3 in the Commemoration,[8] in the *Libera nos* after the Our Father.[9] And, of course, it is found in countless prayers during the season of Advent.

In charismatic renewal, we can see how the hope of the Parousia is expressed in many of the songs that

have been composed in recent years.[10] The same conviction can be seen in the many communities and ministries calling themselves Maranatha.

The Catechism on the second coming

The second coming of our Lord Jesus Christ in glory has,
of course, always been part of the Catholic faith. It is
expressed most obviously in the phrase of the Creed:
'He will come again to judge the living and the dead'. As
just mentioned, this hope is affirmed frequently in the
Church's liturgy.[11] But can it be said that the twentieth
century renewal of the Church promoted by the Second
Vatican Council has been making the Catholic Church
more eschatologlcal?

The answer to this question is found in the new
Catechism of the Catholic Church. At the same time as
the Holy Spirit has been renewing the hope of the
Church through charismatic renewal and other renewal
movements, the Holy Spirit has been guiding the
Catholic bishops and theologians writing the new
Catechism. This is quite a remarkable development.

For a topic that is not often mentioned from the pulpit,
the Catechism contains a quite extraordinary number of
references to the second coming of the Lord. They occur
principally in four places: (i) in Part I on the Creed under
the article 'He will come again to judge the living and the
dead';[12] (ii) also in Part I under the articles 'I believe in
the resurrection of the body'[13] and 'I believe in life everlasting';[14] (iii) in some paragraphs in the opening section
of Part II on the sacraments in general[15] and the final section of Article 3 on the eucharist;[16] (iv) in Part IV on
Christian prayer, section II on the Lord's prayer.[17]

Here I want simply to draw attention to the more striking statements in the Catechism concerning the second coming. The first occurs in the context of the teaching of the Creed that 'he will come again to judge the living and the dead' within a section headed 'The glorious advent of Christ, the hope of Israel'. Here we find a long paragraph on the relationship between Israel's recognition of the Messiah and the second coming of Jesus, that would seem to be the first time that an official teaching of the Catholic Church has addressed this link. 'The glorious Messiah's coming is suspended at every moment of history until his recognition by "all Israel"... The "full inclusion" of the Jews in the Messiah's salvation, in the wake of "the full number of the Gentiles", will enable the People of God to achieve "the measure of the stature of the fulness of Christ", in which "God may be all in all"' (para. 674).[18]

The next two citations speak strongly of the Holy Spirit's role in the preparation of the age to come, and they come in the general sections on the sacraments and the liturgy before the treatment of each sacrament. 'The Holy Spirit's transforming power in the liturgy hastens the coming of the kingdom and the consummation of the mystery of salvation. While we wait in hope he causes us really to anticipate the fullness of communion with the Holy Trinity' (para. 1107). This belongs to the nature of the liturgy that is inspired and permeated by the Holy Spirit of God. The sacramental signs - the baptismal bath, the eucharistic banquet, the anointing with oil for healing - all symbolize and prepare for the glory of the age to come. Thus the celebration of the liturgy will continue until the dawn of that age: 'The Church celebrates the mystery of her Lord "until he comes" when God will be "everything to everyone". Since the apostolic age the liturgy has been drawn towards its goal by the Spirit's groaning in the Church: *Marana tha*!' (para. 1130).

The last citation comes from the final section of the Catechism's teaching on the eucharist, which is entitled 'The Eucharist: Pledge of the glory to come'. Here the Catechism applies the general teaching on the sacraments preparing for the age to come specifically to the eucharist: 'The Eucharist is also an anticipation of the heavenly glory' (para. 1402). 'Whenever the Church celebrates the eucharist she remembers this promise and turns her gaze "to him who is to come". In her prayer she calls for his coming: "*Marana tha*!". "Come, Lord Jesus!", "May your grace come and this world pass away!"' (para. 1403). As we shall see in the next chapter, the Catechism sees a particular significance to the recitation of the Lord's prayer and the petition 'Thy kingdom come' within the context of the eucharist.

These passages from the Catechism bring out the dynamic faith of the Church in the second coming. They bring out the role of the Holy Spirit in producing a dynamic towards the Parousia, a hope in the Church and a longing of the Church. They focus on the liturgical expression of this hope and this longing. It is not simply the hope and the longing of individual believers, but the hope and the longing of the whole Church, the Church on earth, the Church in 'final purification' and the Church triumphant in glory.

In the light of this development in the Church's consciousness, we can see the definition of the dogma of the assumption of Our Lady in 1950 in a new and eschatological light. In this teaching, the Church tells us that Mary, the daughter of Sion and the first believer in her Son, has already reached the destiny for which we hope: 'The assumption of the Blessed Virgin is a singular participation in her Son's resurrection and an anticipation of the resurrection of other Christians' (CCC, para. 966). This doctrine is rightly understood, not separately as another Marian privilege, but as part of eschatology, as an intrinsic element in the Church's hope for the age to come.

As the Holy Spirit makes the Church more eschatological, the Spirit is restoring the fulness of the New Testament hope. This hope is of total salvation, the deliverance of all creation from its bondage to decay, the establishment of the new heavens and the new earth, our resurrection in glorified spiritual bodies, in which there will be total communion with all the saints and angels in the perfect harmony and eternal life of the Most Holy Trinity.

Chapter Ten

The Holy Spirit makes the Church more Eschatological

II: The Our Father

The Holy Spirit makes the Church more eschatological in that it gives the Church her distinctive hope. That hope is summed up in the longing for her Lord to come in glory. Thus, we are told in the book of Revelation: 'The Spirit and the bride say "Come"' (Rev. 22:17). This is the longing of the Holy Spirit. The Holy Spirit desires the fulfilment of all things with the infinite ardour of God's love. So 'Come' is the cry of the Spirit.

The Spirit given to the Church, then, produces this cry in the Church - it teaches the Church to cry 'Come'. So the vision of John is that the Spirit and the bride cry 'Come'. The bride cries out for the bridegroom - not just in her own strength, but in the power of the Holy Spirit.

The age of the Church

The Church as we know it belongs to the period between the first and the second comings of Jesus. The Church of sacraments, the Church of signs, the Church of faith, belongs to this age between the comings. 'The gift of the Spirit ushers in a new era in the "dispensation of the mystery" - the age of the Church, during which Christ manifests, makes present and communicates his work of salvation through the liturgy of his Church, "until he comes" ' (CCC. para. 1076).

The Holy Spirit makes us aware of the tight connection that exists between the gift of the Spirit, the nature of the Church in this world, the form of the liturgy and the sacraments, and the hope of the age to come. The Church exists to embody the hope, to proclaim the hope and pray for the hope. The hope is the full extension of the fruits of the first coming of Jesus to the whole of Israel, to all nations and peoples, and to the whole of creation.

The Our Father

The prayer and longing of the Church through the Holy Spirit is supremely expressed in the Our Father. The Our Father is the prayer that characterises the age of the Church. It is a prayer made in the power of the Holy Spirit that is given to the Christian, and it is a prayer that is directed towards the full coming of the kingdom with the reign of the Christ. It is made with especial force in the eucharistic assembly for, as Vatican II said, 'The liturgy is the summit towards which the activity of the Church is directed; it is also the fount from which all her power flows.'[1] Thus, the Catechism teaches in its section on prayer: 'In the Eucharist, the Lord's Prayer also reveals the eschatological character of its petitions. It is the proper prayer of "the end-time", the time of salvation that began with the outpouring of the Holy Spirit and will be fulfilled with the Lord's return' (CCC, para. 2771).

The first coming is directed towards the second. The resurrection of Jesus cries out for the resurrection of all for whom he died and rose. Faith in the first coming produces hope for the second. Thus the Catechism says of our faith in the salvation accomplished once for all in Christ crucified and risen: 'From this unshakeable faith springs forth the hope that sustains each of the seven petitions, which express the groanings of the present age... The Eucharist and the Lord's Prayer look eagerly for the Lord's return, "until he comes"' (CCC, para. 2772). We can now look at the ways in which the Holy Spirit brings each petition of the Our Father alive in relation to the blessed hope of Jesus' coming in glory.

Our Father. The fatherhood of God is revealed by Christ through the Holy Spirit. The bonds of the Church that enable us to say 'Our Father' are the work of the Holy Spirit. But the Father is the one who has created us for total glory in the coming kingdom. God's fatherhood will be fully realised and fully acknowledged in the wonder of the kingdom when Jesus comes in glory. God's fatherhood will then be fully visible. So when we cry out 'Our Father' now, we begin the acknowledgement that will be total and eternal in the age to come.

Who art in Heaven. As the Catechism says, 'This biblical expression does not mean a place ("space"), but a way of being; it does not mean that God is distant, but majestic' (CCC, para. 2794). Heaven is God's dwelling place; 'the Father's house is our homeland' (CCC, para. 2795). Jesus has gone ahead to prepare a place for us: 'When I go and prepare a place for you, I will come again and will take you to myself, that where I am you may be also' (John 14:3). Already our citizenship is in heaven: 'Our commonwealth is in heaven, and from it we await a Saviour, the Lord Jesus Christ' (Phil. 3:20). So the phrase 'who art in heaven' evokes the awareness that we are called to this heavenly dwelling-place of God. Our Father in heaven: it is he who sends his Spirit from heaven, the Spirit who prepares us to dwell for ever with the heavenly Father.

Hallowed be thy name. Now begin the seven petitions. The first series of three 'carries us towards him, for his own sake: thy name, thy kingdom, thy will!' (CCC, para. 2804). They reflect what Jesus lived out on earth, his passionate desire for the Father's glory, the total orientation of his being to the fulfilment of the Father's will and his mission. 'These three supplications were already answered in the saving sacrifice of Christ, but they are henceforth directed in hope towards their final fulfilment, for God is not yet all in all' (CCC, para. 2804).

'Hallowed be thy name' is a very Jewish expression of worship. For the Jew, sanctifying the Holy Name of God is the holiest duty and the meaning of life. The Name is who God is. That is why the Jews do not pronounce the Name of God, but always use a form of synonym or allusive reference. This phrase expresses the profound reverence of Jesus for his heavenly Father. Hallowed be thy name means that we abase ourselves before the majesty and the holiness of God. It invites us to deepen our reverence for God and the way in which we speak of the Almighty.

Thy Kingdom come. This petition makes more explicit the meaning of 'Hallowed be thy name'. God's name will be perfectly hallowed when God's kingdom comes. God's kingdom will come when the Lord Jesus returns in glory and hands everything over to the Father. The Catechism says: 'In the Lord's Prayer, "thy kingdom come" refers primarily to the final coming of the reign of God through Christ's return' (CCC, para. 2818).

It is the Holy Spirit who prepares the way for the coming of the Lord. It is only through the Spirit that we can cry 'Abba, Father', 'Jesus is Lord' and 'Come, Lord Jesus'. 'Thy kingdom come' does not mean abandoning this world and hoping for a deliverance totally from outside. It means praying for an increase in Jesus' invisible rule now, through an intensification of his presence in the Church, in Christians and in the world, all as preparation and build-up for his return and his visible rule. 'Since Pentecost, the coming of that reign is the work of the Spirit of the Lord who "complete(s) his work on earth and brings us the fulness of grace"' (CCC, para. 2818).

Thy will be done on earth as it is in Heaven. Again, this petition further unpacks the meaning of 'hallowed be thy name' and 'thy kingdom come'. It also looks forward to the coming of the Lord. This petition reaches for the time when all things will be in their right relation to God, when 'the creation itself will be set free from its bondage to decay and obtain the glorious liberty of the children of God' (Rom. 8:21). Total subordination to God will be the most glorious liberty!

However, God's will can only be done on earth as in heaven, when Jesus comes and the heavenly descends to the earth. The final vision of John, the seer of Patmos, is of the holy city, the new Jerusalem, 'coming down out of heaven from God' (Rev. 21:2, 10). In the completion of all things, in the fulness of the kingdom, there will be no separation between heaven and earth, no gap, no abyss between them, as the new heavens and the new earth are brought into being through the resurrection of all flesh. 'For the earth will be filled with the knowledge of the glory of the Lord, as the waters cover the sea' (Hab. 2:14). Then alone will God's will be done on earth as in heaven.

From this perspective, all obedience to God's will on earth is a preparation for the kingdom to come. This fulness to come will not occur through the final removal of the Church from the earth to a celestial sphere, but by the transformation of all things through the resurrection of the dead. Then will the heavenly and the earthly come together under the rule of him who already has 'all authority in heaven and on earth' (Matt. 28:18). Then the goal will be realised: 'Behold, the dwelling of God is with men' (Rev. 21:3).

Give us this day our daily bread. In this petition we ask our heavenly Father for our daily provision, what we need to live this day as his sons and daughters. Bread is the most basic need. The Catechism says: '"Our" bread is the "one" loaf for the "many"' (CCC, para. 2833). It speaks of our solidarity in need. Then the Catechism speaks of 'the specifically Christian sense of this fourth petition' as concerning 'the Bread of Life':

'The Word of God accepted in faith, the Body of Christ received in the Eucharist' (CCC, para. 2835).

It is here that we can see the eschatological sense of this petition. The eucharist prepares us for the banquet of the kingdom; it is the food of pilgrims on their way to the Father's house. The bread we need each day, this day, is to help us on our way: physical bread, the bread from the two tables of the word and of the eucharist. The Catechism brings out this aspect in saying: 'Finally... its heavenly meaning is evident: "this day" is the Day of the Lord, the day of the feast of the kingdom to come' (CCC, para. 2837).

And forgive us our trespasses, as we forgive those who trespass against us. In one way, this petition is the opposite of 'thy will be done on earth as it is in heaven'. This time we are praying that God will act from heaven, as we are acting on earth. The Catechism calls this 'astonishing' (CCC, para. 2838). The mercy of God first touches our hearts to enable us to forgive others. As we yield to this transforming grace, we ourselves are healed.

This petition too arises from the condition of the Church between the comings. In this world, the treasure of the Spirit is poured into earthen vessels. We are weak and we sin. We sin against God and against one another. 'If we confess our sins, he is faithful and just, and will forgive our sins and cleanse us from all unrighteousness' (1 John 1:9). In this world, our relationships are preparing us for the kingdom to come. The communion of the Church is a school for the perfect communion of the kingdom. When we forgive, we are receiving the other, the one who has offended and injured us, as a son or daughter of the Father, called to the same destiny as ourselves. When we forgive, we are saying 'I want you in the kingdom'. 'Forgiveness is the fundamental condition of the reconciliation of the children of God with their Father and of men with each other' (CCC, para. 2844). Each act of forgiveness from the Lord is preparing us for the total reconciliation and acceptance of the kingdom 'in which nothing unclean can enter' (Rev. 21:27).

And lead us not into temptation. Whereas the first three petitions of the Our Father represent an unfolding of what was in the first, the last three lead up to the last 'Deliver us from [the] Evil [one]'. 'This petition goes to the root of the preceding one, for our sins result from our consenting to temptation; we therefore ask our Father not to "lead" us into temptation' (CCC, para. 2846). Temptation is the effort of the evil one to pull us from God's will and God's kingdom.

This petition reminds us that, until the second coming, the Church on earth lives in a situation of conflict. 'We are engaged in the battle "between flesh and spirit"; the petition implores the Spirit of discernment and strength' (CCC, para. 2846). 'The Holy Spirit makes us discern between trials, which are necessary for the growth of the inner man, and temptation, which leads to sin and death' (CCC, para. 2847). We are not to be discouraged by such conflict. St Paul introduces his teaching on this spiritual battle by the exhortation: 'Be strong in the Lord and in the strength of his might' (Eph.

6:10). He ends this teaching with an exhortation to 'pray at all times in the Spirit' (Eph. 6:18) and that he himself might 'proclaim the mystery of the gospel' (Eph. 6:19) and do so 'boldly' (Eph. 6:20). To proclaim the coming kingdom is to expose temptation and to undermine its power.

As with Jesus' victory over the tempter, 'such a battle and such a victory become possible only through prayer' (CCC, para. 2849). But for us, we are united with Jesus and with one another in his body. We have been sealed and marked by the Holy Spirit of God, claimed as the possession of the Father. We have nothing to fear from temptation if we hold firm to the position and the status we have been freely given in Christ. But we are to know that each temptation now is a preparation for the ultimate battle, both our personal ultimate battle before death and the final battle of the Church before the coming of the Lord. 'Finally, this petition takes on all its dramatic meaning in relation to the last temptation of our earthly battle; it asks for final perseverance. "Lo, I am coming like a thief! Blessed is he who is awake"' (CCC, para. 2849). The Catechism speaks elsewhere of 'the Church's ultimate trial': 'The kingdom will be fulfilled, then, not by a historic triumph of the Church through a progressive ascendancy, but only by God's victory over the final unleashing of evil, which will cause his Bride to come down from heaven' (CCC, para. 677).

But deliver us from Evil. 'In this petition, evil is not an abstraction, but refers to a person, Satan, the Evil One, the angel who opposes God' (CCC, para. 2851).

This is the prayer of Jesus for his disciples: 'I am not asking you to take them out of the world, but I ask you to protect them from the evil one' (John 17:15). Jesus is inviting us to share in his prayer. We can only grasp the fierceness of the conflict between the evil one and God as we open ourselves to the Holy Spirit and the life of Jesus.

'Victory over the "prince of this world" was won once for all at the Hour when Jesus freely gave himself up to death to give us life' (CCC, para. 2853). The Catechism then cites Revelation 12, where the 'dragon was angry with the woman, and went off to make war on the rest of her offspring' (Rev. 12:17), seeing this woman as Mary, the new Eve on whom the enemy had no hold. 'Therefore the Spirit and the Church pray: "Come, Lord Jesus", since his coming will deliver us from the Evil One' (CCC, para. 2853).

The final deliverance for which the Church prays will sum up and complete all previous deliverances. 'In this final petition, the Church brings before the Father all the distress of the world. Along with deliverance from the evils that overwhelm humanity, she implores the precious gift of peace and the grace of perseverance in expectation of Christ's return' (CCC, para. 2854).

It is the Holy Spirit and only the Holy Spirit that communicates the meaning of the Lord's prayer to the Church. It is the Holy Spirit that opens up the depths of each petition, as it is the Holy Spirit that enkindles the fire and the longing in the Church for the fulness of the kingdom, and the coming of her Lord.

Chapter Eleven

The harmony of the vision

In the course of this book, I have sought to show how the Holy Spirit is making the Catholic Church more trinitarian, evangelistic, eucharistic, ecumenical and eschatological. As will, I hope, have been apparent throughout, these dimensions of the Church cannot be isolated into separate compartments, but rather all belong together. It may be helpful in this closing chapter to indicate more fully how these different dimensions fit together and in fact require each other for their own authenticity.

First of all, the evangelistic proclamation of the word of God requires the sacramental expression of the gospel of redemption in the eucharist. This has already been covered at the beginning of chapter 4, under the heading 'The eucharist as the gospel enfleshed'. It is the heart of the movement of God for our salvation that the Word becomes flesh. The gospel message proclaimed in evangelisation is then enacted and given in Christ's flesh and blood in the eucharist. The Church becoming more evangelistic is then inseparable from the Church becoming more eucharistic. A deeper reception of the word proclaimed makes possible a deeper celebration of the word made sacrifice for us, which in turn opens us up to receive the word proclaimed at a deeper level.

Then the evangelistic needs ecumenical interaction and expression. As was indicated in chapter 3, we Catholics need to learn something vital from the Evangelicals and the Pentecostals in order to evangelise more effectively. What we have to learn focuses on the preaching of the death and resurrection of Jesus as the ground for the death-resurrection experience of conversion. What they can learn from us is how the full fruit of the gospel they proclaim requires its enfleshment (incarnation) in the eucharist. However, they will only be able to receive this as we become more authentically evangelistic and they can recognise the power of the Holy Spirit in our proclamation. They need convincing evidence that our focus on liturgy and sacraments does not represent a ritualistic bondage that obscures rather than reveals the reality of Jesus Christ.

The evangelistic also requires the eschatological. First, in the sense that the promise and hope of the second coming and the resurrection from the dead are part of the good news of the gospel that we must proclaim. We do not simply proclaim forgiveness of sins now and heavenly life for the soul after death. We proclaim the full good news of the final deliverance from all forms of evil in the resurrection of the body. We proclaim God's promise of the new heavens and the new earth. God's work of salvation embraces all levels of God's creation, for all levels have become tainted by the disease of sin and its consequences. Secondly, the preaching of the gospel hastens the coming of the Lord. There is a correlation between the evangelisation of the world and the day of the Lord's return. 'And this gospel of the Kingdom will be preached throughout the whole world, as a testimony to all nations; and then the end will come' (Matt. 24:14).[1]

The eucharist requires the ecumenical, because the eucharist symbolises the wedding feast of the Lamb to which all the redeemed are invited. 'Thus from [eucharistic] celebration to celebration, as they proclaim the Paschal mystery of Jesus "until he comes", the pilgrim people of God advances, "following the narrow way of the cross", towards the heavenly banquet, when all the elect will be seated at the table of the kingdom' (CCC, para. 1344). The oneness of our Christian hope (see Eph. 4:4) provides the deepest reason why the reconciliation of divided Christians is an urgent necessity and why our inability to celebrate together at the table of the Lord is such a grave scandal. A deeper grasp of the eucharist as the memorial that makes present in the power of the Holy Spirit will intensify the one hope for the wedding feast of the Lamb. As the Holy Spirit communicates to all Christians a deeper sense of the Church being prepared for the feast of the kingdom, the Holy Spirit will open the way to a greater sharing in holy communion.

The ecumenical also requires the eschatological. Again, the grounds are the same as for the eucharist. 'There is one body and one Spirit, just as you were called to the one hope that belongs to your call' (Eph. 4:4). What is this hope? It is 'our blessed hope, the appearing of the glory of our great God and Saviour,

Jesus Christ' (Tit. 2:13). Every work of the Holy Spirit is preparing for the coming of the king and his kingdom. If the divided churches are obeying the Spirit of God in any way, they are being led to the same destination. It is only because we limit the corporate vision of our churches to this present age that we can imagine separate denominational and ecclesiastical futures. Further, all our churches and traditions are deeply challenged by the Lord's dealings with Israel and the history of the Jewish people. As our repentance extends beyond simple anti-semitism, which it must include, we will be led to a repentance for the ways in which we have dejudaised Jesus, the Twelve, Mary and the New Testament. It is here that our common repentance will lead the separated Christian churches and communities into previously unimaginable forms of unity, as we rediscover our common foundation in the natural olive tree of Israel. This reorientation will necessarily restore with a new clarity the one hope of the coming of the Messiah and the messianic kingdom that is so central to the faith of Israel - the hope that did not end with Jesus, but was advanced and deepened by his whole life and ministry.

I have alluded here and there to the importance of the role of Mary, the Mother of God, but I have not devoted a chapter to the Holy Spirit making the Church more Marian. This, perhaps, is not only due to the time limitations in the retreat for which these teachings were prepared, but also for a deeper reason - the same reason that I have not treated of the Holy Spirit making the Church more ecclesial. For the renewing work of the Holy Spirit, particularly through the Second Vatican Council, has highlighted the depth of the bonds between Mary and the Church. 'At once virgin and mother, Mary is the symbol and the most perfect realisation of the Church' (CCC, para. 507).[2]

As the Holy Spirit makes the Church more evangelistic, more eucharistic, more ecumenical and more eschatological, each aspect will include a Marian dimension. The evangelistic and the ecumenical will manifest more the purifying work of the Holy Spirit, so that the Church's belief concerning Mary stands forth in greater clarity within the full biblical revelation, while the eucharistic and the eschatological will bring forth the full depth of God's workings in the elect, both Mary and the Church. The deepest sense in which the Holy Spirit is making the Church more Marian is the bringing of the Church towards its eschatological perfection that Mary already enjoys: 'The mother of Jesus, in the glory which she possesses in body and soul in heaven, is the image and beginning of the Church as it is to be perfected in the world to come' (CCC, para. 972).[3]

All of the four dimensions treated - evangelistic, eucharistic, ecumenical and eschatological - have a trinitarian character. All can only be advanced through the Spirit of God, all involve a deeper revelation of the incarnate Son of God and all lead us in Christ through the Spirit to give glory to the Father. All lead us into deeper fellowship with one another in the body of Christ. This fellowship is necessarily fellowship in the Holy Spirit, and leads us into the glorious sonship of the children of God.

In all these dimensions, there is a coming together of the witness of the scriptures, the teaching of the magisterium and the experience of renewal in the Spirit. As the Holy Spirit makes the Church more trinitarian, the Holy Spirit is increasing the richness of our diversity and deepening the bonds of unity. Being made more evangelistic, eucharistic, ecumenical and eschatological is to be expanded by the Creator-Spirit. In charismatic renewal, we have experienced the rediscovery of spiritual gifts - gifts of healing, prophecy, praying in tongues and, we hope, discernment of spirits. Through all the modern movements in the Catholic Church, there has been an opening up to the gifts of lay people, thereby making the ministry of the ordained more a service of equipping and energising the whole body. Through the opening up of the scriptures we experience an expansion of horizon, the richness of revelation, the unfathomable depths of our God and of the mystery of his Son. All this is a preparation for the kingdom, for which the Holy Spirit is preparing the whole body of Christ, and not least the Catholic Church. 'But, as it is written, "What no eye has seen, nor ear heard, nor the heart of man conceived, what God has prepared for those who love him", God has revealed to us through the Spirit' (1 Cor. 2:9-10).

Appendix

Official documents on evangelisation and initiation

This appendix provides references to the documents of the magisterium relating to initial proclamation and evangelisation, as well as an account of their development over the last thirty years. It provides a more detailed account of official Catholic teaching than was given in chapter 2, where the focus was on a simple presentation of the main developments relating to initial proclamation of the gospel in the process of Christian initiation. So it was not mentioned in chapter 2 that there is a difference between the use of the term evangelisation in the Rite of Christian Initiation of Adults (RCIA) from the Vatican Congregation for Divine Worship (1972)[1] and that in the General Directory for Catechesis (GDC) from the Vatican Congregation for the Clergy (1997).

Evangelisation in the RCIA

In RCIA, the term evangelisation is restricted to the initial proclamation of the gospel. As we shall see, this is what is called 'initial proclamation' in the GDC and some other official documents. Thus, the first phase in the process outlined in RCIA is called 'Period of evangelisation and precatechumenate'. 'It is a time of evangelisation: faithfully and constantly the living God is proclaimed and Jesus Christ whom he has sent for the salvation of all' (para. 36).

Evangelisation is directed towards conversion. 'From evangelisation, completed with the help of God, come the faith and initial conversion that cause a person to feel called away from sin and drawn into the mystery of God's love' (para. 37). At the end of the evangelisation or precatechumenate, RCIA presents the first step on the road to baptism and full participation in the life of the Church: 'Acceptance into the order of catechumens'.[2] The RCIA document makes clear that this step is not to be taken until there are clear signs of a personal response to the proclamation of the gospel: 'There must be evidence of the first faith that was conceived during the period of evangelisation and precatechumenate and of an initial conversion and intention to change their lives and to enter into a relationship with God in Christ' (para. 42). There 'must also be evidence of the first stirrings of repentance, a start to the practice of calling upon God in prayer, a sense of the Church and some experience of the company and spirit of Christians through contact with a priest or with members of the community' (para. 42).

The catechumenate that follows, the time of formation of the candidates or catechumens, deepens the initial faith and the initial conversion resulting from the evangelisation: 'the dispositions manifested at their acceptance into the catechumenate are brought to maturity' (para. 75).

Evangelisation in the GDC

In the GDC, the term evangelisation refers to the whole process from the first impact on the unbeliever through all the steps leading to baptism to the life-long formation of each Christian. The concern here seems to be twofold: first, the insistence that there needs to be constant proclamation of the gospel throughout our lives. We never graduate to a point where we no longer need to hear the basic gospel and move on to higher things. Secondly, there is the concern, first clearly articulated in Paul VI's letter on evangelisation, to ensure that evangelisation is not conceived in a simplistic manner limited to individuals, while having no impact on culture and society. 'But evangelisation would not be complete if it did not take account of the unceasing interplay of the gospel and of man's concrete life, both personal and social' (*Evangelii nuntiandi*, para. 29). Paul VI had spoken of 'the complex, rich and dynamic reality which is called evangelisation' (para. 17), on which the GDC elaborates: 'Evangelisation... must develop its "totality" and completely incorporate its intrinsic bipolarity: witness and proclamation, word and sacrament, interior change and social transformation' (para. 46).

The GDC, however, clearly speaks of the first phase of explicit proclamation that corresponds to what RCIA calls evangelisation or precatechumenate. In several places, the GDC describes the different stages or phases of Christian conversion and initiation. The wording varies from one instance to another, but the stages are clearly identifiable. I have tried to tabulate them in a way that makes their distinctiveness clear:

Para. No.	Preliminary	Phase 1	Phase 2	Phase 3
47	Christian witness, dialogue and presence of charity	The proclamation of the gospel and the call to conversion	Catechumenate and Christian initiation	Formation through the sacraments
49		Missionary activity to non-believers and religiously indifferent	Initial catechetical activity to those who choose the gospel	Pastoral activity to the Chistian faithful of mature faith
61-70		Primary or first proclamation (61)	Catechesis (63)	Continuing education in faith (69)
88		The pre-catechumenate	Catechumenate followed by a stage of purification and illumination	Mystagogy (experience of the sacraments)

The second column provides the references to the 'initial' or 'primary' proclamation. The initial proclamation, as in RCIA, leads to initial faith and initial conversion.

The other documents of the magisterium

The GDC of 1997 was in many ways developing more fully an understanding of evangelisatlon and initial proclamation that had evolved in the Catholic Church after the publication of the RCIA. The principal documents that treat of these matters are the Apostolic exhortation *Evangelii nuntiandi* of Paul VI (1975); the post-synodal document on catechesis, *Catechesi tradendae* (1979) and the encyclical *Redemptoris missio* (1990), the last two being from John Paul II.

Evangelii nuntiandi. Paul VI's was a pioneering message. It was this letter that put evangelisation clearly on the agenda of the Catholic Church. As mentioned above, Paul VI was aware of the complexity of evangelisation. He began the process of enlarging this concept from that in the RCIA. Paul VI stated clearly that 'the purpose of evangelisation is... precisely this interior change, and if it had to be expressed in one sentence the best way of stating it would be to say that the Church evangelises when she seeks to convert' (para. 18). For this transformation, it is necessary that Jesus Christ be explicitly proclaimed: 'The Good News proclaimed by the witness of life sooner or later has to be proclaimed by the word of life. There is no true evangelisation if the name, the teaching, the life, the promises, the Kingdom and the mystery of Jesus of Nazareth, the Son of God, are not proclaimed' (para. 22).

Thus, in one sentence, Paul VI suggests both the rich complexity of the task of evangelisation and points to its unique centre in Jesus Christ. However, he does not speak directly of the first proclamation, and so there remains an ambiguity in the way he juxtaposes the words 'kerygma, preaching or catechesis' in para. 22.

Catechesi tradendae. Here the distinction of the basic kerygma from subsequent catechetical teaching is clearer than in *Evangelii nuntiandi*. In fact, their distinctly different purposes are explained with as great a clarity as anywhere: 'The specific character of catechesis, as distinct from the initial conversion-bringing proclamation of the Gospel, has the twofold objective of maturing the initial faith and of educating the true disciple of Christ by means of a deeper and more systematic knowledge of the person and the message of our Lord Jesus Christ' (para. 19).[5] As this post-synodal document is concerned with catechesis, it does not say more on initial proclamation. However, it clearly uses the term 'evangelisation' for the entire process of Christian formation, as it describes catechesis itself as a moment in the 'whole process of evangelisation' (para. 18).

One other point worth noting from *Catechesi tradendae* is its reference to actual situations that fall well short of the ideal. In practice, the Pope says, 'the initial evangelisation has often not taken place' (para. 19). This paragraph lists several categories of Catholics being presented for catechesis who have not personally given themselves to Jesus Christ: children baptised in infancy who come for catechesis without any other initiation and who have no personal attachment to Jesus Christ; unbaptised children whose parents later present them for catechesis; many baptised pre-adolescents and adolescents who have been given systematic catechesis and the sacraments but are hesitant about commitment to Jesus Christ; adults who doubt or abandon their faith (para. 19).[6]

Redemptoris missio. This encyclical letter of Pope John Paul II addresses the missionary work of the Church, and it is in this context that it addresses the issue of evangelisation and initial proclamation. While the Pope acknowledges that the missionary task of the Church is universal, and knows no geographical limits, this document nonetheless specifically addresses missionary work 'within well-defined territories and groups of people' (para. 37).

This encyclical presents its own order of Christian initiation, which focuses on the Church's mission of implanting the gospel in unevangelised areas and sectors of life:

Witness (paras 42-43)
The initial proclamation of Christ our Saviour (paras 44-45)
Conversion and baptism (paras 46-47)
Forming local churches (paras 48-50)
Incarnating the gospel in people's cultures (para. 52-54)

The first category of witness refers to the importance of the way of life of the missionary, the Christian family and the ecclesial community (para. 42). This is regarded as 'the first form of evangelisation'. But then the Pope is very clear about the necessity of a distinctive initial proclamation before catechesis: 'Initial proclamation has a central and irreplaceable role, since it introduces man "into the mystery of God, who invites him into a personal relationship with himself in Christ" and opens the way to conversion' (para. 44).

In this encyclical, the Pope says more about proclamation than is said in the other documents.[7] The subject of proclamation is Christ. Proclamation is never merely an individual act, but is always made in union with the entire ecclesial community. Proclamation is inspired by faith. Faith produces a boldness in proclamation. What is proclaimed is not just a human truth, but the 'Word of God'. The highest form of proclamation is the witness of martyrdom.[8]

Catechism of the Catholic Church. There is no section of the Catechism, and no index entry, on evangelisation.[9] The first relevant entry is in the prologue: 'While not being formally identified with them, catechesis is built on a certain number of elements of the Church's pastoral mission which have a catechetical aspect, that prepare for catechesis, or spring from it. They are: the initial proclamation of the Gospel or missionary preaching to arouse faith; examination of the reasons for belief; experience of Christian living; celebration of the sacraments; integration into the ecclesial community; and apostolic and missionary writings' (para. 6). The main references to the proclamation of the gospel come in the section on Jesus Christ in paras 425-429. The distinction between initial proclamation and catechesis is implicit, rather than explicitly taught, in the separate paragraphs on preaching and proclaiming Christ (para. 425) and catechesis (para. 426).[10] The teaching on the Church's missionary calling (paras 849-856), which comes within the section headed 'The

Church is Catholic', hardly mentions proclamation. There is one paragraph on the lay role in evangelisation under 'Participation in Christ's prophetic office' (para. 905), which speaks of evangelisation as 'the proclamation of Christ by word and the testimony of life', which is itself a quotation from *Lumen gentium*. The last section on forms of consecrated life has a heading 'Consecration and mission: proclaiming the King who is coming' (before para. 931). This appears to be the only place where proclamation is directly related to the eschatological hope, which otherwise is strongly present and developed in the Catechism.

Notes

Introduction

1 'The "study of the sacred page" should be the very soul of sacred theology' (Vatican II, Constitution on Divine Revelation, *Dei verbum*, para. 24).

2 *Dei verbum*, para. 10.

3 Para. 25.

One

1 In Eucharistic Prayer no. III, the celebrant prays before the consecration, 'We ask you to make them [these gifts] holy by the power of your Spirit, that they may become the body and blood of your Son, our Lord Jesus Christ' and after the consecration, 'Grant that we, who are nourished by his body and blood, may be filled with his Holy Spirit, and become one body, one spirit in Christ.'

2 'The mystery of the Most Holy Trinity is the central mystery of Christian faith and life. It is the mystery of God in Himself. It is therefore the source of all the other mysteries of faith, the light that enlightens them' (para. 234).

3 'In it [Christ's resurrection] the three divine persons act together as one, and manifest their own proper characteristics' (para.648).

4 Part 1, section 2, article 9, para. 2, immediately before para. 781.

5 Part 2, section 1, chapter 1, article 1, immediately before para. 1077.

6 See the summary of these headings in para. 1112.

7 The question of unity and diversity will be looked at in more detail in chapter 6.

Two

1 Paul tells Timothy to 'do the work of an evangelist' (2 Tim. 4:5).

2 'The Paschal mystery of Christ's cross and Resurrection stands at the centre of the Good News that the apostles, and the Church following them, are to proclaim to the world' (CCC, para. 571).

3 'I bring you good news of a great joy which will come to all the people; for to you is born this day in the city of David a Saviour, who is Christ the Lord' (Luke 2:10-11).

4 The term 'evangelisation' is used in *Ad gentes*, paras 6, 14, 23, 27, 30, 35, 38, 39 and 41. In para. 17, the decree states 'there are so few clerics to evangelize such great multitudes'. It also occurs in the Decree on Bishops, para. 6, but is not found in the Constitution on the Church.

5 This idea is present without the terminology of 'new evangelisation' in the Apostolic Exhortation *Christifideles laici* (1988), in which John Paul II says of areas where 'many vital traditions of piety and popular forms of Christian religion are still conserved', '... only a re-evangelisation can assure the growth of a clear and deep faith' (para. 34). The term new evangelisation is then used in the encyclical *Redemptoris missio* (1990) in paras 2, 30, 33, 34, 83, 85 and 86.

6 Part III of the Directory is entitled 'The Pedagogy of the Faith', of which chapter 1 is 'The pedagogy of God, source and model of the pedagogy of the faith'. Para. 140 on 'the pedagogy of Christ' has its own description of the process: 'receiving others: proclamation of the kingdom; a love that liberates from evil and promotes life; an invitation to a manner of living'.

7 The Decree on Ecumenism says that 'in Catholic doctrine there exists an order or "hierarchy" of truths, since they vary in their relation to the foundation of the Christian faith' (*Unitatis redintegratio*, para. 11).

8 Constitution on the Liturgy (*Sacrosanctum concilium*), para. 64.

9 *Redemptoris missio*, para. 44.

10 This word is not much used in the official Catholic documents, though it does appear in *Catechesi tradendae*, para. 18.

11 We continue to need proclamation to grow in faith. Hence every liturgy involves proclamation of the word. But this theme is not developed here, as our subject is primary proclamation.

12 *Sacrosanctum concilium*, para. 35.2.

13 Ibid., para. 29.

Three

1　Chapters 6, 7 and 8 directly address the ways in which the Holy Spirit is making the Church more ecumenical.

2　Oasis grew from 7,000 to 20,000 members between 1974 and 1976.

3　RELaY stands for Reconciliation among Christians, Evangelisation, Lay leadership formation and Youth mobilisation

4　Holy Trinity, Brompton is an evangelical Anglican parish, which had been impacted by the charismatic movement for over twenty years - in a rather low key way.

5　Nicky Gumbel *Questions of Life*, p.22.

6　Of course, Catholics recognise that there have been remarkable conversions in the course of Christian history produced by an unexpected grace of God, beginning perhaps with Saul of Tarsus on the road to Damascus, but including figures like St. Augustine of Hippo, St Ignatius Loyola, Blaise Pascal and Charles de Foucauld.

7　There has, in fact, been intense debate among Evangelicals about whether spiritual revival can be planned, as Charles G. Finney believed, or whether it can only be prepared for in prayer. But it remains true that Evangelicals, though strongly activist, generally emphasise the unpredictability and divine origin of revival.

Four

1　The phrase 'the bread of God' appears in John 6:33.

2　Constitution on the Liturgy, *Sacrosanctum concilium*, para. 10.

3　Ibid., para. 26.

4　Ibid., para. 7.

5　It is out of this conviction that the teaching of the Constitution on the Liturgy states: 'The principal manifestation of the Church consists in the full, active participation of all God's holy people in the same liturgical celebrations, especially in the same Eucharist, in one prayer, at one altar, at which the bishop presides, surrounded by his college of priests and by his ministers' (para. 41).

6 Eucharistic Prayer III.

7 CCC, para. 1396.

8 See 1 Cor. 2:16; Phil. 2:5.

9 This is not the place to discuss the relationship between ordained and lay forms of teaching, or to provide a Catholic reflection on the teaching ministries of pastors and leaders in other churches and streams of renewal. My concern here is that such teaching is deeply needed, and that it is an essential component of the ordained ministry of bishops, priests and deacons.

10 1 Tim. 4:6, 11, 13; 6:3; 2 Tim. 1:13; 2:24–25; 4:2–3; Titus 1:9; 2:1–10, 15.

11 Mark's Gospel particularly makes this link between preaching and the manifestation of evil: see Mark 1:21-27.

12 Cardinal Joseph Ratzinger with Vittorio Messori, The *Ratzinger Report* (San Francisco: The Ignatius Press, 1985).

13 In recent years, more Catholic dioceses have appointed priests as diocesan exorcists, and at the same time an international association of Catholic exorcists has grown in numbers and significance.

14 Michael Perry (ed.) *Deliverance: Psychic Disturbances and Occult Involvement* (London, 1996: SPCK) and *A Time to Heal: A Contribution towards the Ministry of Healing* (London, 2000: Church House Publishing).

15 At the end of the year 2000, the Vatican Congregation for the Doctrine of the Faith issued an Instruction on prayers for healing, that particularly concerns healing ministry within the liturgy.

Five

1 *Sacrosanctum concilium* para. 8, also cited in CCC, para. 1090.

2 From preface of Masses of the Holy Eucharist, I.

3 See Heb. 8:2.

4   Para. 7.

5   See Heb. 3:1; 4:14; 6:4; 8:5; 9:23-24; 12:22-24.

6   Heb. 7:7.

7   See Heb. 7:24, 26; 9:24.

8   Lev. 16:14-15, 18.

9   See also Lev. 1:11, 15; 3:2, 8, 13; 4:5-7, 16-18, 25, 30, 34;
    5:8-9; 8:15; 9:8-9, 18.

10 See Eph. 4:8; 6:12; Col. 2:15; 1 Peter 3:22.

Six

1   Instruction *Ecclesia Catholica* of the Holy Office dated December
    20, 1949.

2   *Unitatis redintegratio*. para. 3. The next sentence says: 'For the
    Spirit of Christ has not refrained from using them as means of
    salvation which derive their efficacy from the very fullness of
    grace and truth entrusted to the Catholic Church.'

3   The English translation was called *Divided Christendom* and came
    out in 1938. Fr Congar was made a cardinal in 1994 at the end
    of his long life.

4   *Unitatis redintegratio*, para. 8.

5   The only churches where there is little identifiable charismatic
    renewal are those which have opposed it and sought to expel or
    marginalise adherents. The relation of the Orthodox Church to
    the charismatic movement is more complex and this is not the
    place to address this question.

6   Sometimes other terms are preferred for this foundational
    experience/grace of charismatic renewal. Some prefer to speak
    simply of being filled with the Spirit.

7   For example, the late Nelson Litwiller, a prominent Mennonite
    leader in the USA, received through the ministry of Catholics;
    Charles Whitehead (Catholic, UK) received through the ministry
    of an Anglican priest; two French priests, both founders of
    communities, Fr Laurent Fabre and Fr Bertrand Lepesant,
    received through an American Episcopalian.

8   There have, of course, been some other ecumenical influences that have impacted the popular level. One thinks in particular of the Taizé community in France, and perhaps also the Focolari movement. These exceptions all have a strong spiritual dimension.

9   I addressed the reasons for this lack of interaction in an article '*Ut unum sint* and the Charismatic Movement', E*cumenical Trends* 27/7 (July/Aug 1998) 13-16.

10   Here I should pay tribute to the work of Fr Kilian McDonnell, OSB, over many years in urging Catholic charismatics not to be isolated from wider Church concerns and theology, and in urging fellow-theologians to pay more attention to the Pentecostal-charismatic phenomenon.

11   The most significant achievement has been the Joint Declaration on Justification signed by leading representatives of the Catholic Church and the Lutheran World Federation at Augsburg on 31st October, 1999. To date, this is the only document issuing from a theological dialogue to lead to an official joint declaration of the churches sponsoring the dialogue.

Seven

1   *Unitatis redintegratio*, para. 3.

2   Ibid., para. 6.

3   Declaration of 7th December, 1965.

4   The French original was entitled *Pour la conversion des églises*. An English translation, *For the Conversion of the Churches*, was published by WCC Publications in 1993.

5   The document studies in turn Christian identity, ecclesial identity and confessional identity, before examining Christian conversion, ecclesial conversion and confessional conversion.

6   *Briefing* 30/4 (12 April 2000), p.3.

7   'Memory and Reconciliation', a document of the International Theological Commission in *Briefing* 30/4 (12 April 2000) I, I, I, p. 9.

8   Printed in *New Covenant* 7/4 (October 1977) p.10.

9   See John Dawson, *Healing America's Wounds* (Ventura, Ca.: Regal, 1994). The British Anglican, Russ Parker, prefers to speak of 'representative confession'.

10 Their application to the division between the Church and Israel will be examined in chapter 8.

11 For example, 'the enemy has destroyed everything in the sanctuary' (Ps. 74:3); 'O God, the heathens have come into thy inheritance; they have defiled thy holy temple: they have laid Jerusalem in ruins' (Ps. 79:1). See also Ezekiel 19.

Eight

1 In the Decree on Non-Christian Religions, *Nostra aetate*, para. 4.

2 Address of Pope John Paul II in the synagogue of Rome, 13th April, 1986.

3 There were already some 'Messianic Jews' in Israel before the movement began in the USA, as in Israel the formation of a Hebrew-speaking Church of converted Jews was a natural consequence of forming an 'indigenous church'.

4 For example, an early seventh century document from Toledo, Spain, states 'how we were long and rightly constrained to sign this Declaration... to support the Catholic faith: we therefore make these promises... undertaking for the future not to become involved in any Jewish rites or customs nor to associate with the accursed Jews who remain unbaptised ... we will not practise carnal circumcision, or celebrate the Passover, the Sabbath or the other feasts days connected with the Jewish religion.'

5 The Hebrew Catholic Association produces a magazine entitled *The Hebrew Catholic.*

6 See *Tertio millennio adveniente*, para. 18.

Nine

1 The New Testament text, both in 2 Cor. 1:22 and in Eph. 1:13 has the gerund form of the verb, not the noun *sphragis*. The gerund indicates an active movement, not just the bestowing of an object.

2 See 1 Cor. 9:27; 10:1-13; Gal. 5:4, 21; Phil. 3:18-19.

3 The Greek for 'promised Holy Spirit' reads *tō pneumati tēs epangelias tō hagiō*, literally 'with the Holy Spirit of promise'. It makes more sense to understand the promise as referring to the future, namely the Holy Spirit that is promised, that brings the

promise, rather than referring to the past. Where the Holy Spirit given now is the Spirit promised in the past, (through Ezekiel, John the Baptist).

4 'A seal is a symbol of a person, a sign of personal authority or ownership of an object. Hence soldiers were marked with their leader's seal and slaves with their master's' (CCC. para. 1295).

5 Here again some of the translations are misleading. RSV has 'the guarantee of our inheritance until we acquire possession'. But it seems much more appropriate to understand the 'possession' being acquired by God. God is marking us with his seal of ownership, but God does not acquire full possession until the resurrection.

6 The Greek of Heb. 9:28 has the noun *form*, literally 'he will appear to the ones awaiting him for salvation' (*eis sōtērian*).

7 For example, 'Christ has died. Christ has risen. Christ will come again'; 'Dying you destroyed our death, rising you restored our life. Lord Jesus, come in glory'; 'When we eat this bread and drink this cup, we proclaim your death, Lord Jesus, until you come in glory.'

8 '... ready to greet him when he comes again'.

9 '... as we wait in joyful hope for the coming of our Saviour, Jesus Christ'.

10 For example: 'I am the Bread of Life'; 'Lion of Judah on the Throne'; 'There is a Redeemer'. Also in two songs of Graham Kendrick: 'There's a Sound on the Wind' and 'This Is My Beloved Son'.

11 This is especially true of the liturgies of the Eastern churches.

12 Article 7, paras 668-682.

13 Article 11, paras 988-1019; see especially para. 1001.

14 Article 12, paras 1020-1060; see especially paras 1021, 1038, 1040 & 1041.

15 See in particular paras 1090, 1107 & 1130.

16 Paras 1402-1405.

17 To be treated in chapter 10.

18 The passages cited bring together Paul's teaching in Rom. 11:12, 25–26; Eph. 4:13 and 1 Cor. 15:28.

Ten

1   *Sacrosanctum concilium*, para. 10.

Eleven

1   See also 2 Peter 3:9.

2   'She is the "exemplary realisation" (*typus*) of the Church' (CCC, para. 967).

3   From *Lumen gentium*, para. 68.

Appendix

1   The RCIA was first restored in 1972 with the original Latin edition of which there was a slight revision in 1974. The official English-language translation came out in 1987 and incorporated some changes required by the new Code of Canon Law of 1983.

2   It is in this rite of admission to the order of catechumens that the candidate is marked with the sign of the cross. There are six very expressive formulae provided to accompany the signings: (i) Receive the cross on your forehead. It is Christ himself who strengthens you with this sign of his love. Learn to know him and follow him; (ii) Receive the sign of the cross on your ears, that you may hear the voice of the Lord; (iii) Receive the sign of the cross on your eyes, that you may see the glory of God; (iv) Receive the sign of the cross on your lips, that you may respond to the word of God; (v) Receive the sign of the cross over your heart, that Christ may dwell there by faith; (vi) Receive the sign of the cross on your shoulders, that you may bear the gentle yoke of Christ.

3   This paragraph refers to the RCIA. In line with the GDC presentation of evangelisation, it replaces the RCIA language of 'evangelisation and precatechumenate' with that of 'the precate chumenate, characterised as the locus of first evangelisation leading to conversion and where the kerygma of the primary proclamation is explained' (GDC, para. 88).

4   The term 'mystagogy' was used in the early centuries by the Fathers of the Church. It is also called 'post-baptismal catechesis' (RCIA, p.14; para. 306). Mystagogy refers to the experience of 'the mysteries', meaning baptism and the eucharist, as personal experience of a mystical communion in Christ and his

body.

5   See also: 'Thus through catechesis the gospel kerygma (the initial ardent proclamation by which a person is one day overwhelmed and brought to the decision to entrust himself to Jesus Christ by faith) is gradually deepened, developed in its implicit consequences... ' (para. 25).

6   The GDC also acknowledges: 'Frequently, many who present themselves for catechesis truly require genuine conversion' (para. 62).

7   The following statements are all found in para. 45, except the first, which comes from para. 44.

8   This reference to martyrdom is a hallmark of the thinking of John Paul II, who has introduced teaching on martyrdom into several of his encyclicals, notably *Veritatis splendor* (1993) on moral teaching and *Ut unum sint* (1995) on ecumenism.

9   There is an index entry on 'Proclamation of the gospel'.

10   The distinction is in some way present in para. 429, which says that 'this loving knowledge of Christ' gives rise to 'the desire to proclaim him', to 'evangelize', and then later that 'the need to know this faith better makes itself felt'.